Native Wisdom
of a
Soulful Leader

Understanding the Three Core Elements
to Access the Leader Within

Delvina Waiti

GOWOR
INTERNATIONAL PUBLISHING

Native Wisdom Of A Soulful Leader: Understanding the Three Core Elements To Access The Leader Within© Delvina Waiti 2016

The moral rights of Delvina Waiti to be identified as the author of this work have been asserted in accordance with the Copyright Act 1968.

First published in Australia 2016 by Gowor International Publishing

www.goworinternationalpublishing.com

ISBN 978-0-9944581-6-2

Any opinions expressed in this work are exclusively those of the author and are not necessarily the views held or endorsed by Gower International Publishing.

All rights reserved. No part of this publication may be reproduced or transmitted by any means, electronic, photocopying or otherwise, without prior written permission of the author.

Disclaimer

All the information, techniques, skills and concepts contained within this publication are of the nature of general comment only, and are not in any way recommended as individual advice. The intent is to offer a variety of information to provide a wider range of choices now and in the future, recognising that we all have widely diverse circumstances and viewpoints. Should any reader choose to make use of the information herein, this is their decision, and the author and publisher/s do not assume any responsibilities whatsoever under any conditions or circumstances. The author does not take responsibility for the business, financial, personal or other success, results or fulfilment upon the readers' decision to use this information. It is recommended that the reader obtain their own independent advice.

Testimonials

Delvina has always been an insightful, thoughtful and intuitive leader. As a soulful leader, she empowers others through a leadership methodology that draws on a deep understanding of cultural leadership. In working with Delvina, I have seen her belief in native wisdom, as a powerful teacher and guide, transform perspectives and outcomes for leaders, teachers, students and communities.

Throughout reading *Native Wisdom of a Soulful Leader*, I was challenged to consider how my academic and innate leadership could be improved with a more soulful approach. In particular, the link between soulful communication and relational trust highlighted the connections Delvina is making between academic theory and native wisdom. My perspectives were yet again challenged, and this book proved to be an exceptional reminder of the power of leadership and the importance of including a soulful lens when conducting introspective reflection.

Native Wisdom of a Soulful Leader will challenge your perspectives and open your mind to new possibilities and alternative outcomes.

Ben Clapp ~ Assistant Principal

Every now and then you come across a person whose presence you feel way before you set eyes on them. Then when you turn around to look, you are stunned by seeing the "Mana" that they carry.

This is my experience of Delvina. She encapsulates a wisdom and knowing from such a deep space that you feel what she has to share comes from a place of experience, resonance and leadership.

Her book *Native Wisdom of a Soulful Leader* shares the core of what today's leaders everywhere need to embody.

Being from her homeland, Aoteroa, I felt that the knowledge flowing through is supported from a long line of ancestors – and she captures the true essence which re-ignights what the soul is longing to share.

Te Mana – Spirit; Te Mauri – Impulse; Te Maui – Insight are what each of us desires to call forward and to that end, Delvina has shared, in simple but deep terms, her journey back to ourselves.

Thank you for decoding the mystery surrounding the true meaning of leadership, Delvina. Anyone who reads this book will be touched and inspired to step into their own role, be that as mother, father, teacher, counselor and anywhere that true Leadership is required. Which is in most areas of life. You are changing the way in which we are inspired to live, work and play.

Anyone who reads your book will remember who they truly are and how they can embody that easily for their part on the planet.

Luanne Mareen ~ Goddess on Purpose

As I began to read *Native Wisdom of a Soulful Leader* I couldn't stop reading. I was drawn into the powerful message within the pages. I could feel the passion in Delvina's writing about what she believes in and how she perceives life and what it has to offer. Delvina's openness, honesty and hope for a better future is evident. An excellent read that leaves the reader with much to think about and act on.

Kiri Dewes ~ Maori Elder

Delvina, a true Soul leader herself, will not only inspire anyone who reads her book, *Native Wisdom of a Soulful Leader* to engage in some deep reflection and consideration of her comprehensive and beautiful exploration of what is a soulful leader, but also empower them with the practical tools to explore and embody soulful leadership.

The world needs every soulful leader — individuals, teachers, parents, those in business and in any position with leadership expectations to remember, step into and embrace their innate and natural soul leadership.

Soulful leadership is our responsibility to the generations that follow us. It's reach and ripple effect is desperately needed. Thank you for stepping into your soulful leadership to bring us the inspiring blend of *Native Wisdom of a Soulful Leader*.

Melissa Rowe - Mindful Mamas.

Dedicated to...

To my amazing family, I am glad we chose each other to ride the soul train together.

Personal Note From The Publisher

Hi there!

As the Founder of Gowor International Publishing, my publishing house, I make it part of my practice to offer a personal review for my authors about their book. The reason I do this is so that you, as the reader, can glean a further understanding into why this book is about to become a valuable part of your life.

There is no doubt that a high number of books have been written on the topic of leadership from various authors around the world. Each book shares insights on how a person can become a 'better' leader in their workplace or life, how they can raise their level of influence, and how they can lead people in teams or movements more powerfully. And, while many of these books are undeniably valuable, many of them lack what I feel this book has: deep cultural roots in ancient wisdom on the topic.

In *Native Wisdom Of A Soulful Leader*, Delvina shares profound principles and concepts that will take both your definition and understanding of leadership to a new depth and help you to become an extraordinary leader in whatever capacity you desire. As you read through the chapters, you will become immersed in the ancient wisdom that, once deeply understood and applied, will assist you to bring your soul through every action and word that you speak as a leader: an essential key to having a greater impact in the world.

Every time I speak with Delvina, I feel more connected to the essence of who I am as she reminds me that being authentic is one of the most powerful things we can do in order to touch hearts and open minds. Delvina is real, heartfelt and grounded – three powerful qualities that great leaders embody – ... and she inspires me. Her commitment to people unfolding their true potential is moving and today I am deeply inspired that you have this book in your hands as I know that you are about to experience the great gift of Delvina's presence that I have had the blessing of receiving.

I know that you will enjoy the book the same way that I did...

It's time to wake up the soulful leader within you!

With inspiration,

Emily Gowor

Founder of Gowor International Publishing

TABLE OF CONTENTS

Foreword 6
A Different Kind of Leadership 9
PART 1 - Leading From Within 15
    Chapter 1: Leadership 17
    Chapter 2: Soulful Leader 29
PART 2 - The Shift 43
    Chapter 3: Earth's Evolution 45
    Chapter 4: Aligning With The Collective Consciousness 53
PART 3 - Native Wisdom of Leadership 63
    Chapter 5: Native Wisdom of Life 65
PART 4 - Te Mana 73
    Chapter 6: Spirit – The Feminine 75
PART 5 - Te Mauri 89
    Chapter 7: Impulse – Te Mauri – The Union 91
PART 6 - Te Maui 101
    Chapter 8: Insight – The Masculine 103
PART 7 - The Blueprint 117
    Chapter 9: Understanding The 3 Core Elements 119
    Chapter 10: Activating The Three Core Elements for Leadership 129
PART 8 - The Experience 141
    Chapter 11: Experiencing The Soul Connection 143
    Chapter 12: The Soulful Journey Begins 153
Author and Divine Guidance Message 160
Acknowledgments 162
About The Author 163

Foreword

Delvina Waiti is my favourite niece (everyone's a favourite with me). She is one of my sister Diane's daughters and a joyful wee soul, whose progress I have followed with great pride since her birth many years ago.

She asked me to write this foreword because she is aware of my long association in kapa haka, leading Ngati Rangiwehi for 35 years and as former Rotorua deputy mayor and councillor for 38 years.

She figured I might know a thing or two about leadership.

After reading this book *Native Wisdom of a Soulful Leader* I was absolutely blown away by her intellect and the wairua (spirituality) she expressed.

My view of leadership is simple. A leader should lead by example. The best leaders are those who do that in a quiet and dignified way, achieving great results by bringing people along with them on the journey.

I've worked with many people like that over the years. Each brought their own into leadership.

I think of the late Sir Peter Tapsell, former councillor, Member of New Zealand Parliament and Speaker of the House, who encouraged me to get into local government politics at a young age. The respect Sir Peter received was as a direct result of his leadership abilities. He earned respect in the way he led.

In the Maori world, I think of the many wise elders on the Awahou Marae and our river that flowed from Taniwha Springs in Rotorua, where I was brought up.

The late Pakake Leonard, our chief of Ngati Rangiwehi in the 1970s and 1980s, demonstrated outstanding leadership amongst his people and non-Maori at a difficult time.

He showed his mana by keeping us strong and together against huge odds, e.g. thousands of acres confiscated from our tribe.

He was firm with me and others in the tribe, and as Rotorua deputy mayor, he stood up to others in local government.

Both men dressed impeccably and showed dignity when others would show anger.

If someone asks me what soulful leadership is, the simplest way to describe it is that you treat people as you would want to be treated yourself.

All good leaders have that trait. They may not call it soulful leadership, but it is.

Delvina captures that brilliantly in this book. While she has lived in Australia for many years, she has not lost that spiritual link to her ancestors and whanau (family).

Leaders like Sir Peter and Pakake are the reason for that. They, and those who came before them over many centuries, laid the foundations for the next generation. This has allowed Delvina to express her individuality and as a result, she has written a beautiful book which I implore people to read.

Ma te atua koe e manaaki Delvina (God bless you my, niece Delvina).

Cr Trevor Maxwell

A Different Kind of Leadership

I want to open your mind to a different kind of leadership, a way to look at yourself through the ancient perspective of leadership as a birthright. You are born to lead your life; no one else can do it for you but you. This is an old as time paradigm, so why is the most common question asked about leadership... "Are we born to lead, or do we learn to lead"? The simple answer to that question is, "yes." Our natural birthright is to lead our own lives to fulfil our destiny (I wish it were that easy), and along the journey of our lives, we pick up valuable experiences (good and bad) that enable us to learn more about our type of leadership and the way we want to live our lives.

I'm going to open your mind further to the ancient perspective of leadership and its true essence. Leadership = Life, and you are the master of your universe. How you lead is a measure of how much you value life, and how you live is how well you lead. It's a simple concept, yet we still haven't mastered the simplicity of Leadership and Life. There is a simple reason why we miss the concepts of Leadership and Life, and that is a lack of clarity around our purpose or why we do what we do. The ancient perspective on purpose always came back to your birthright. You are born for a reason, for a mission, and it is your leadership to become clear on your purpose or your why. The greater your leadership is around clarifying your purpose, the greater your life journey becomes and the more you will value life.

The purpose does not always resemble grandeur missions or make history books (you never know, yours might), but the purpose is the soul's connection to the leader within, and the leader within all of us is connected to a greater infinite source.

Awakening This Soulful Leader

I have always been passionate about leadership, but didn't realise it until I began showing up in the world as a "Kid Coach." In 2008, I began my first Children's relaxation and self-worth group, teaching children how to meditate and use strategies for calming anxiety. I started this as an afterschool program as I was still a full time teacher in Primary School. This business grew popular and extended into personal coaching for kids dealing with parent separation and victims of violence. I loved this work and began leading wellbeing programs within my school and presenting at a Wellbeing Conference how to bring these teachings into a school. I was showing up in my world and making an impact on the children I taught.

In 2011, I left the education industry as a leading teacher to have my fourth child, and I returned to the teaching industry as an education consultant in mindfulness. Going back into the profession as a consultant was not as impactful as being the teacher in the classroom. I felt teachers did not have the confidence to continue mindfulness within their classroom routine, so I decided to pursue my love of leadership and encourage other professionals and business owners to stand out, be seen and heard as the soulful leader they are born to be and the soulful leader the world needs. Using ancient Native Wisdom to unlock their potential to create and lead from a soulful perspective.

Native Wisdom

An ancient Maori narrative, the creation story of the universe is the background I have used to extract the gold nuggets of soulful leadership. This knowledge that once was only privy to the ancient ones under Tohungaship (shamanism) or the like, is now coming into the light for awakened leaders to endeavour. While I know that narratives can be interpreted in different ways, I have included my experiences and exactly how to activate the leader within that allows anyone to become a soulful leader.

Growing up, I identified with being indigenous and stereotyped as a lower class minority. My parents knew that the way to a rich culture was through education and always supported my higher learning. I trained as a Primary School Teacher in New Zealand and continued a Masters in School Leadership degree, and an Executive Positive Psychology certificate in Australia, where I currently live. For so long (or so it feels), I have neglected my innate native wisdom being here in Australia. It seemed that there was no room in education for me to explore this as a part of who I am. I also wondered how many children feel the same way in the education system?

Being involved in various groups outside of teaching, most of them spiritual, I was able to explore the other half of me that I left dormant for so long. I explored my native wisdom through the channel of meditation, healing trance from amazing teachers and divine guides. Each teacher and guide kept my native wisdom pure, knowing that what I was learning then was preparing me for now. Since following an entrepreneurial journey, I have been encouraged to be all of me and bring all facets of myself to my own leadership forefront. I own my native wisdom and the uniqueness of its origins, for it is merely a way to explain that we are all one and belong to the same conscious collective. I chose to be indigenous in this lifetime so I could inspire leadership change from the foresight of ancient native wisdom. I chose to be here now to be in a soulful leadership revolution.

Making the Most of the Wisdom

If you haven't noticed, I am very spiritual but extremely practical. I need to be practical because I am a spiritual being living a human existence. I am a mother, teacher and entrepreneur trying to make an impact in the world with my message. I am here because I chose to be, and I chose to impart this wisdom on to you through this book. I absolutely trust in Great Spirit and divine timing of how, when and why things happen in life, and this book is one of those trust in the divine decisions. I have had an overwhelming urge to get this book out of me, and when I sat with this desire and connected to my soul, the words and divine wisdom flowed like a river. When I got into the flow of writing (and it took about a month), I did not want to stop. I couldn't wait for the next writing episode to connect with divine wisdom and explore native narratives. As I wrote, I could feel the transformation in a profound way. I understood the wisdom better than when it was locked in a special room within my heart.

To experience this profound transformation, as I did, you only need to open your heart to the divine wisdom spread throughout the pages. Throughout this book you will see divine messages written in italics. These are guides that wanted to channel divine messages to you as I was writing. So where they are is how they came through. Not all the guides were the same, as I felt different energies through different messages. As the book explored deeper realms of soulful wisdom, the vibration lifted and the guides changed. You will feel this within the book, especially when you try the exercises or activate the three core elements. It is important that you take what you need and leave what you don't. We are all experiencing a human existence, and we are all on different spiritual paths, whether we accept it or not. Let yours be a soulful one and let it begin right here.

There are no mistakes, as Oprah would say, and there is no mistake that this book is in your hands. You are meant to read something within the pages that will resonate with you. I don't know what it might be, but you will. I urge you to let the words sink into your being. Take what you need or what you agree with and let the wisdom guide you. There is deep wisdom etched into these words, but simplicity is the theme. My husband doesn't read books, and I asked him, "When I become a published author will you read my book?" He laughed and said of course, so I have written this with him in mind. Keep it simple or he wont read it. If you are a leader of a business, company, organisation or family (so anyone willing to show up in the world in a profound way) then this book is for you.

Leadership is such a journey in itself, and to have the tools to enable you to lead from a soulful place will ensure profound transformations for you and the people you lead. I have discovered my soulful leadership journey not within the industry from which I worked for over 10 years, but through my own entrepreneurial journey. The business journey that I have embarked on has opened my heart from the inside out and allowed me to be the leader that I was born to be. I have been given the chance to bring my gifts to the world, in my unique cultural way. Being indigenous Maori has given me the values and wisdom to look beyond the physical and go into an innate wisdom that each being on this planet posseses. This innate wisdom is the leader within.

This book will take you on an inward journey to your innate wisdom and connect you to the soul of your leadership. It is a leader's guide to achieving soulful leadership. The content within this book will challenge your thought leadership, solve leadership hurdles and get to the soul of who you are as a leader. The book will guide, teach and, most of all, transform you on a profound level as a leader, as it has done for me through my experiences as an educational leader and an entrepreneurial leader. The information on these pages is much more than just words from my leadership experience, but also comes from native wisdom from my culture and divine channelled guidance. This is not your average leadership theory text book-type learning; rather it is for leaders who are looking for an alternative way to lead that nourishes their soul and gives them a greater sense of purpose from which to lead. These leaders are looking for a practical guide that is easy to understand and simple to implement and most of all, gives them the *conviction, courage and confidence* to lead soulfully.

I wrote this book with the intention of providing aspiring leaders, teachers in the education industry, an alternative to the norms of educational leadership. Teachers looking to lead from within so their integrity and soulful wisdom is intact. However, when writing this wisdom, it has transpired through divine guidance as a guide for all aspiring leaders in all walks of life. My stance on leadership has always been one that does not always require a job description, but can be leading your family as a mother or father, leading a community group, leading your own business or leading an organisation. I have been turned down from online leadership groups because of my leadership belief and scoffed at by a boss.

The truth is leadership is challenging you every single day of your life no matter what it is you do professionally or personally. Leadership is how you show up in the world and the message that you are sharing for the greater good of humankind. I know that when my leadership beliefs are being challenged and make some feel uncomfortable in "leadership roles," I am on the right path, and my conviction grows in courage and the confidence to stand out and be heard.

PART 1

Leading From Within

Chapter 1: Leadership

*"Leadership is no longer about your position.
It's now more about your passion for excellence and making
a difference.
You can lead without a title."*
Robin Sharma

Leading is something we are all innately born to do. This is such a contradictory statement, as everything on leadership I have learnt or read says no one is a born leader. Believe it or not, everyone has the capability to lead. If you break it down, we all lead in some way. We lead our own lives, our children, and our families. We make decisions and we take action; after all, we are living life. So does that mean if you are living you are leading? Interestingly enough, I say yes.

Go with me on this for a while…if I was to say we are all born leaders ready to take the helm of any ship that needs our navigation skill, would you think that to be correct? Well, of course, there are many levels to leading, and it would take some special skills to navigate a ship, but the point is anyone and everyone has the capacity to be a leader.

Soulful Leaders are mirrors for those that aspire to lead. Leading does not have to be of many followers or work related. It can be as simple as how you soulfully lead your family to school in a calm and timely manner. It could be how your friends admire your compassion or your capacity to make great partnerships. When you become an inspiration for others to do better for themselves, that makes **you** a soulful leader. Inspiring a better way to live or be is a soulful leader in the highest and purest form.

PART 1 - Leading From Within

I want to breakdown some of the leader misconceptions and look at it from a human perspective. I have attempted to give you **my** explanation of a leader. These two words are similar but have very different meanings.

Leader

An exceptional human being, willing to show up in the world to share a message and make a difference.

Leadership

The capacity and skill set to navigate your message to the world in a way that inspires growth and positive change.

Leadership Challenges and Values

The most challenging problems modern leaders face within leadership can be classified in two parts: external challenges and personal challenges. The external challenges are the crises or problems that arise around the leader within and around the organisation, such as interpersonal problems, economic and political problems just to name a few. The personal challenges are the challenges the leader faces from within. These personal challenges or leader limitations are fear, lack of confidence, egocentric and lack of empathy, which make the task of implementing change a difficult one.

External and personal challenges can cause symptoms of STRESS. Leaders invest high levels of emotion in their jobs, and if not dealt with or supported, these lead to stress and in turn create more personal challenges for leaders. For the content of this book, I am solving the personal challenges of the leader within through the three core elements and minimising the symptoms of stress. I have developed a model for soulful leader change implementation that solves the external challenges, and I will share how to do this in the next soulful leader book. Great leaders in history lead with these three personal values:

Courage to be authentic in their vision and speak their truth.

Confidence in bringing their vision into the world.

Conviction in their beliefs and values.

The Three Cs (values) are a strong foundation of the leader within and are part of some of history's most successful transformational leaders. However, there are misconceptions about being a leader and leading from within. I have listed the 5 most common misconceptions about being a leader:

1. Leave yourself at the door before you lead, become someone else or hide behind a mask.
2. No room for emotion in leadership; it is seen as weak.
3. My way or the high way.
4. Leaders are charismatic and out there.
5. Leaders are infallible and don't make mistakes.

We have these misconceptions because of the historical nature of past leaders and eras. It is more so our assumptions that a particular leadership style that suited someone else will suit our leadership purpose too. Well, it doesn't. There are so many factors that need to be taken into account. Who are you serving? What do your followers want? Does it make you feel good? Does it light you up? Most of the time, leadership misconceptions are all related to the fact that we are not ourselves. We become someone behind the mask. It's interesting to look at leadership from this perspective because it is not looked at from a deep inward journey to self.

I studied a Masters in School Leadership and learnt a lot about leadership styles and the theory of leadership. The course tried to get deep and inward by looking at your leadership wounding experiences, which is a great place to start, but without the self-development tools to guide you through these experiences and beyond, leaders continue to make the same mistakes in different guises. True leadership is discovering the type of leader you are within, your message and gifts, and whom you are inspiring with your message or gifts. I'm not just talking about leadership styles either. I'm talking about the uniqueness of you as a leader. Taking a journey of self-discovery will help you to see your true potential and how you will inspire others through the gifts you have to share through your leadership.

Leader = born with gifts or a message to share.

Leadership = skills to navigate and motivate others with their gifts.

So... If everyone is a leader, then why is this world in such a state of affairs? Well, let's be honest. I didn't say we all lead in the right way. In fact, many misuse their leader powers for their own gain, manipulation and pleasure. It's plain to see in the history of the world's tyrant leaders that power and manipulation are leadership fundamentals. I guarantee these leaders do not have a happy endin. In fact, they signed their own fate when they choose to embark on a leadership that does not inspire others through positive change. Instead they inspired others to follow a way that is not in the best interest of all mankind. Our own human existence in history talks of different leaders and without getting too technical and historically heavy on you, I will sum them up in 4 eras.

Prehistoric Era

Leader/Warrior/Hunter

This leader's sole purpose was to provide food, shelter and safety for his tribe. Tribesman followed him because of his warrior strength and stealthlike hunter abilities. He inspired others to survive and led them to hunt and fight.

Ancient Times

Leader/Philosopher/Writer

This leader used insightful knowledge and theories about the world around him and humanity. He gathered followers with his elegant use of words and or literature. He inspired others with his mind and led through his teachings.

Middle Ages

Leader/Negotiator/Conqueror

This leader's sole purpose was to gain power, prosperity and freedom for his kingdom. His powers of negotiation included linking pure bloodlines and arranged marriages to powerful families and kingdoms. He led armies to victory and sometimes to defeat. He inspired others to fight for glory and freedom.

Modern Era

Leader...

Honestly, this is where it becomes confusing. The modern era leader is all of the above and more. He is transformational and he is a tyrant. He has weapons of mass destruction and his words have the ability to move masses. He is a global conqueror and negotiator, hunting down his next revolution. The modern leader is so muddled by leadership theory and contradictions, learning from perceived anecdotal causes and effects, which is purely hearsay. Society has moved into an information era. We are now leaders of the 21st century with knowledge and an audience at our fingertips. But this does not make leadership any easier. For a 21st century leader it is competitive, and it's harder to stand out with so many others competing to be seen and heard.

PART 1 - Leading From Within

Technology has given us the platform to get to the masses, and it's all ready at the push of a button. It's so easy to start a revolution or movement and gain followers just from being in front of your computer screen. Gone is the industrial age where working harder, doing the same thing and increasing output was a gage of your potential and leadership ability. The 21st century has challenged us to find smarter and more creative ways to do things. Adding value and solving problems innovatively are high performing requirements. Along with these challenges, we have less time to create the solution, and autopilot does not work in the 21st century. We cannot find a one-fits-all solution and do the same thing day in and day out.

The Soul and Shade of Modern Leaders

The modern era leader and the soulful leader have a choice. (I am choosing to talk in the masculine to illustrate this message, but it can be feminine too). His role is not bequeathed to him; he chose it because he believes in something. Because he has a strong belief in himself and his cause, he becomes an inspiration to those that follow. When he is inspiring to others, he can connect his cause to a wider audience by taking his message globally. And the catch is this leader could have "soul" or "shade." If this modern leader chooses soul, he will be a great transformational leader, inspiring those who follow to grow and change with his development. If a modern leader chooses shade, he will be a great tyrant leader, inspiring others to believe in his message and follow him unwaveringly to his demise. If you notice, both leaders are inspirational in different ways, but their messages come from different places and their followers are kept at different levels.

Soulful Leader = bring followers to their level (inspire leadership in others).

Shade Leader = keep followers at his command (no inspiration to go beyond his leadership).

I'm going to break this down a little further...

Soulful Leader – works with love for his followers, inspiring them to be like him or better.

Shade Leader – works in fear, not allowing anyone to better him or take his leadership. He instils fear when he commands.

Just a little further...

Modern Leaders

Soulful (Transformational) = LOVE

Shade (Tyrant) = FEAR

When you see the modern leader for what they are, it is easier to sort through the anecdotal fluff and get to the essence. Now the choice is yours. There is a tonne of information and books written on transformational and tyrant leadership, but I like to break this stuff right down and use my own simple terms. Feel free to delve a little deeper into some of the leaders that exhibited these leadership traits. I know you could easily think of a few right now just from the above explanation. Just to name a few...

LOVE	**FEAR**
Luke Skywalker	Darth Vader
Gandhi	Hitler
Martin Luther King	Pol Pot
Nelson Mandela	Saddam Hussein

It may not seem like tyrant leaders have fear, but their behavioural characteristics operate from a fear-based perspective.

PART 1 - Leading From Within

www.emotionalcompetency.com/tyranny.htm has a great leadership and tyranny chart to compare the behavioural characteristics of the two leadership traits.

Soulful leaders do come from a place of love, but it does not mean they do not have fear or elements of shade, which I like to call shadows. Soulful leaders have shadows that they need to work through. These shadows are what hold soulful leaders back from their true potential and doing their heart's work. Shadows have the ability to inhibit energetic flow and harmony. When shadows are present, leaders may come across as being incongruent with what they say and do or just not quite right. Being aware of shadows is essential to work through things and let them go to bring in new energy and flow. I will talk more about shadows later in this book.

Leadership Toxicity

If you are operating as a soulful leader, beware of leadership toxicity and getting caught in its web. In my experience, I have found this to be in two parts. Your leadership becomes toxic 1: If you are or change through ego and self-righteousness; and/or 2: Others' perception of you has changed due to their own jealousy and ego. Have you ever heard anyone say things like, "Give them a little power and it goes straight to their head," or, "They think they are so high and mighty"? Leadership toxicity is due to one powerful and yet detrimental thing... Ego!

Ego is the common variant in the two scenarios above. It is either personal ego or others ego. The toxicity that we talk about in ego comes from the energy that ego creates. When we come from a place of ego, what is attached to that energy is fear, jealousy, resentment, hate and distrust, to name a few. It then becomes obvious that when coming from an egocentric leadership point of view, it will unleash toxic energy. The toxic energy stirs emotional upheaval, and this can come from the leader himself or from his followers or workers. That energy is what creates toxic cultures in work places and families.

Leadership + Too much EGO = Toxic Leader + Toxic Cultures (community)

Don't get me wrong, ego is not all evil. It is essential for leadership, but it needs to be kept in check. Ego is needed for confidence, but we do not need massive doses of it.

Ego has the power to make or break you. Let's talk about ego. Ego is essentially driven by fear. Most egotistical leaders have a false sense of pride and a distorted self-righteous image of themselves. The fear is allowing others to see the doubt they have in themselves, so they build up their image with ego and start believing in it. This ego- and fear-driven leader sees himself as the centre of the universe and puts his own agendas first, disregarding others thoughts and feelings. Sound familiar?... Ego in big quantities is definitely Shade Leadership.

Shade Leadership + EGO (lots of it) = FEAR
(This equation also shows the outcome of this leadership style and his followers. Followers will follow out of FEAR).

Ego is not all doom and gloom; it does have the power to "make you," as does fear. These energetic components are needed for leadership in small checked quantities. Let's start with ego. To be an effective leader, you need your egocentric self to step out into the spotlight and help you believe in your choices and why you are leading this particular group to wherever you are going. I like to think of this ego as my conviction. Conviction is about believing in your truth and the purpose of your leadership for the greater good of all. When using your ego as your belief or conviction tool, you are not feeding your ego false images or messages. It is pure belief in you from

PART 1 - Leading From Within

a purposeful perspective. I must say it's not easy to keep this ego in check either; it's so easy to sway very close the shade. Only a small amount of egocentric play is needed for this leadership.

Now let's talk about how fear can be effective in leadership. Just like ego, we need small amounts of fear. These two energetic components work hand-in-hand as fear and ego can be one in the other. Fear is a way of keeping us challenged. It's similar to an adrenaline junkie who searches for his next big thrill. Using fear helps you to stay on the "edge" of your game, wanting more. Fear has the capacity to keep you moving forward on the path you want so much to travel, and it has the capacity to make you turn away from it. Large amounts of fear make dreams and aspirations so hard to achieve and small amounts of fear keep you moving towards them. Counterintuitive, I know. But what I have learned is these two energetic components really can work in your favour as a leader or aspiring to reach your goals and dreams.

My biggest fear in anything I pursued was ego! I was so fearful of becoming egocentric when attaining what I wanted, which meant I never pushed myself forward into the light of my dreams. I did not want to become "big-headed" or have people not like me. When I think about it, I feared FEAR itself. It took a lot of work for me to get used to coming to my edge, which meant accepting fear and seeing it as a measure or stepping stone to achieving what I wanted. I became friends with ego instead of hiding it. I realised when I hid my ego I became somewhat false in how I projected myself onto others. By this, I mean others could see my fears of self-doubt and self-worth. I did not have strong leadership connectedness and people were not willing to follow me. I got help to become friends with my ego and could finally see how ego worked in my favour. What I learned was...

Ego

1. Too much ego leads to tyranny and a "big head."

2. Not enough ego leads to no inspiration for others to connect with you.

3. Small amounts of ego lead us to conviction in our beliefs and purpose.

Fear

1. Too much fear leads to not attaining your dreams and aspirations.

2. Small amounts of fear keep you on edge and wanting more.

So...

The Soulful Leader Formula

Soulful Leadership + ego/fear (very small amounts) = CONVICTION & LOVE

(Followers will follow this style because they LOVE what this leader stands for).

Chapter 2: Soulful Leader

"Great leadership usually starts with a willing heart, a positive attitude, and a desire to make a difference."
Mac Anderson

Soulful leaders are unique beings. A soulful leader is not always a person in a powerful position, but a leader of his or her own life and how they live it to reflect a greater purpose than themselves. You could be a CEO of a company or a mother taking care of a family. They have remarkable instinct, or gut instinct if you like, about certain situations and people. These leaders have absolute compassion for others, especially when a humanitarian cause is at play. Soulful leaders are the new leaders of a new conscious world. An evolved world where consciousness and new age thinking is the norm and a necessary part of living and leading. It certainly does not mean these leaders need to be shamanic or clairvoyant, yet it helps, although these leaders do require a deep understanding of self and a deep sense of purpose in what they do and why they lead.

This deep, soulful self-awareness is the key to leaders leading from a different space than the conventional industrial revolutionary leader. The industrial leader is concerned with more output, money or product for minimal input if possible. If you are a soulful leader and you are in the corporate industry or any organisation that runs on an output based structure, I bet you are feeling empty, unsatisfied and unfulfilled. There was probably a time where you threw yourself into your work and loved working your way up the ladder, but when you got there, the view wasn't what you thought it would be... am I right?

I know this feeling too well. I loved working in the education industry as a primary school teacher, and I was damn good at it. I put my head down and worked hard to work my way up the ladder. In a short time I was leading teams and projects that were satisfying and eventually got promoted to an executive class within my school. While I was overjoyed and thrilled to be in this position, I felt this type of leadership did not suit my soulful design. I definitely loved leadership, but did not find deep enough "whys" or bigger visions that could keep my soulfulness thriving. I also realised I needed some deep inner work of my own to step into an authentic place where I felt free to open up to questioning the big "whys." I needed "Courage" to begin having authentic conversations about the "whys."

The soulful leader is more concerned with the *why?* Soulful leaders have the courage to initiate conversations about why are we doing this or why does it feel this way? And it usually needs to be answered with a deep, purposeful resonance. When leadership is brought forth from a deep sense of self and conviction, visions and decisions come from a place of purposeful clarity. There is a leadership mechanism that becomes totally intuitive or gut instinctive. Clarity, vision and decision are soulful leaders' greatest assets. They will not have all the answers, but they do have an internal mechanism that will eventually tune them into the right path to solve problems. Even if the problem does not turn out the desired way, they see the clarity and lesson in each path travelled. These are the true gifts of soulful leaders, and having a soulful leader leading any organisation or home will make remarkable energetic shifts that everyone can benefit from. If you are a soulful leader in your home, you can create absolute love and harmony.

The Shadow of a Soulful Leader

Our personality as described by Carl Jung, a Swiss psychologist, has two parts: The Persona and The Shadow. Our persona is our everyday mask that we allow others to see. It's how we decide to show ourselves in our world. Our shadow, however, is the part of ourselves that we try very hard to keep hidden, keeping it in the shadows of light. Our shadow is full of all the things we don't want to be or show to others, our fears and our insecurities. We usually disown this part of ourselves and shove it into the deep dark depths of our psyche. The unusual thing about disowning and hiding your shadows is they show up without you realising it through your leadership actions.

Everyone has shadows including soulful leaders. Shadows in leadership can make or break a leader, and the sad thing is, most leaders are unaware of their own shadows, and do not or will not acknowledge they exist.

Soulful leaders have worked deeply on knowing their purpose, why they do what they do and their personal characteristics, but shadows can still linger under the skin. The main shadow of a soulful leader is projection. Projection is a cover up to hide a shadow that we do want to present to others. This is a mask soulful leaders may project out or onto others. This can be a very unconscious thing and only noticeable when it is reflected back to you through a comment or action.

As a teacher, I was always seen as the calm and Zen-like Master that would not step on an ant for fear of it being a reincarnated relative, but it was far from the real me. One colleague would say to me, "Oh, what are you learning about today, Mrs Waiti, butterflies and sunshine?" She knew the real me and would say this to have a chuckle because she knew I didn't like the stigma. The real me got angry, is loud and chaotic. I guess I liked having a Zen-like perception of me, but it didn't help when I began taking on leadership roles and I wanted to roar. I was fearful of breaking down this projection because people might not like me or think I had changed since I became a leader. So I would play it safe and not show my true potential or the real chaotic person I can be. Playing it safe was a big downfall.

PART 1 - Leading From Within

When I left teaching to begin my business, I tried to shift the Zen Master stigma. I swung to the opposite end of the pendulum in hopes people didn't think I was too "woo-woo." So I shut this side of me down, still not being my true authentic self. Consciously I projected another mask that was coming off utterly incongruent to who I was, and people could feel that something was just not right.

The other main block a soulful leader needs to be mindful of is not a shadow, but more so plays off our shadows. That is our thoughts. Being in our headspace too much can have a detrimental effect on our ability to lead well as soulful leaders. The headspace takes us away from going internal with our thought processing and intuition or gut instinct. Being in a constant headspace means we are constantly on the outside of our bodies, losing the ability to feel and sense within. Half of the time, we waste energy on thinking about things that cannot be changed, that haven't happened yet or that will never happen, only to be left feeling worse, depressed and sick.

Over processing or analysing a situation, conversation or action in your head does not serve you unless you have the soulful ability to see other points of view within the given situation. To reflect rather than replay is a soulful way to progress from that particular situation. Soulful leaders are intelligent beings with amazing gifts that need to be shared with the world, but their amazing minds can be their worst enemy. I can guarantee it will always be their own thoughts that get in the way of their true potential.

This is a constant battle I have with my thoughts. I am a big thinker, a big visionary and I used to overwhelm myself with fear and self-doubt. It took a lot of transformational work to overcome fear and self-doubt. Now I keep these two shadows around when I need to be on my edge (just a little, not too much), and they help me move forward now rather than hinder or block me. I'll tell you how later in the book.

I honestly thought there was a mask or hat that you had to put on for the different roles you played in life. In fact, my parents and society taught me this unconsciously in general. My parents were unconscious of this as this is how they were brought up too. Many leaders keep their leadership separate to their lives, especially if they have families. They have a leadership mask and that could be a hardball-type attitude and then they change when they get in the comfort of their own home. What I have discovered after some deep inner work is that these masks are false projections that we put up to keep us safe or protected. But these masks we put up actually use up tireless energy and cause us more harm. If you are putting all your energy into being something that is not your authentic self or something that you do not fully believe in, it is going to drain you of so much energy, you will burn out and your relationships with those you cherish will suffer. These masks are projections. They are projections that take time and energy to keep up appearances. After a while, others will notice there is something not quite right or incongruent about a masked leader.

The Soulful Leader Calling

Soulful leaders hear, feel and see their calling or mission in this world. The calling is so strong it resonates deeply within the leader, and it is almost impossible to ignore. There are leaders who will know exactly what their calling is, and some who will have no idea but feel an alluring urge to pursue *something.* Being authentic to yourself as a leader is taking action to find out what the calling might look like if it hasn't presented itself to you. You may have already had a vision and know what your mission is and how you will achieve it.

For me, I have seen a vision of me speaking on stage and teaching people. I wasn't sure what it was I would be speaking about or even teaching until the urge to write this book came to me. Being on purpose with your

PART 1 - Leading From Within

mission or calling in life is a divine and tremendous feeling. Simply put, when you are on purpose with your mission, you love what you do. You even love the challenges that present themselves because you know the challenges will bring you closer to your goals. I have been following my calling for many years and have understood the little things I have done in my life have prepared me for what's to come. My teaching profession has prepared me to teach Soulful Leadership. Delivering presentations and organising events had prepared me for what's coming.

Identifying Your Calling

Exercise #1

What are the things you are passionate about, or have real conviction about? When you think of it, it will strike a note in your heart. Note these things down in your journal. Think about your journey in life and your career. Note down the things that you have done to prepare you for the things you are passionate about. Create a mind map that links all the things that have prepared you for something bigger.

_____

_____

_____

Even though you may be following your calling or mission, it may not stay the same over time. What I mean is, as you work through your mission, you grow and learn with it. So naturally there is an evolution to your mission too. My mission in this life is to be an advocate for children's wellbeing. I have done this through teaching and establishing businesses that work with alternative wellbeing for children. As I developed through my career and in business, I have recognised a need to develop the knowledge of teachers and parents so they have the skills needed to nurture the wellbeing of children as well as themselves. Even as I write this book, my journey is changing and morphing into opening more people up to a soulful leader way of life through Native Wisdom. This knowledge or gift has a ripple effect that not only helps the soulful leader along their journey, but also helps those around them including family, friends and colleagues.

I didn't do this alone and come up with it all by myself; I sought help from friends, mentors and coaches. I told friends what I wanted to do in my business to keep myself accountable. I sought advice and expertise from coaches to unscramble the overwhelming assortment of ideas in my head. With the help of coaches or mentors, it is not hard to unpack what your calling might look like in the world or how you will share it to a wider audience. Mentors and coaches see your value, gifts and messages for this world. It is up to you to decide which mentors or coaches you resonate with. If you want to work with a mentor or coach, know exactly what kind of person you want to work with.

I personally wanted to work with a coach that was open to energy and the workings of the universe. I also wanted someone who could wade through my headspace of creativity and ideas, and be able to organise them into priority and action lists. I also wanted someone who was honest and would tell me if something wasn't going to work. I have had many mentors and worked with three coaches throughout my entrepreneurial journey, and I'm not finished yet. I will always get help to bring my mission and message to the world in an impactful way.

If you decide that you want to work with a coach to help you find your calling or action your mission, then I urge you to know exactly the kind of person you want to work with. Make sure you feel a resonance with whom you choose to work with. Some mentors and coaches can be too concerned with materialistic outcomes and that's okay, but it's only part of the journey to a point; it may not be your deepest value or vision. Hold your

PART 1 - Leading From Within

vision firm as only soulful leaders can and know what does not sit right with you is okay, and move forward in your vision and in your energetic wisdom.

You are the leader...(a divine message)

You have a calling that cannot be ignored. This calling comes from a higher source and a grand place. It may feel grandeur and large, but it is a collective vision, and we will send others to lift these visions to a higher consciousness. Keep the vision strong and know help is here in many forms. Forms of beauty, musical, peaceful and connected moments can also be teachers. Follow in this path and all forms of help will be given to you. Understand that flow is harmonious intention and blocks are detours to get back onto the path. Your vision is always lit and is a beacon to attract more goodness and love to you. We all have a calling to work for and with each other. Your vision is needed to help others fulfil their calling and this is the collective conscious.

Well, that pretty much so said it better than I could have tried. I do love how divine guidance jumps into this book when I'm writing; it's the best way to write!

The Soulful Journey

My journey began when I was very young. I would always be given messages in the world of dreams. My youngest and most vivid dream was when I was about seven years old, and I would have a reoccurring dream of swimming with an eel. This eel was no ordinary eel. It had Maori designs (ta moko) on its skin and it was enormous. I would always be swimming with this monstrous eel in a crystal clear channel, and it felt warm and wonderful. I had no fear of this animal. Yet in real life, I am terrified of them. In fact, every time we went fishing or to the beach back home in New Zealand, I would always attract eels... yuck!

I was about 12 years old when I was listening to my Koro (grandfather) telling my dad about the eel in Lake Okataina that had a moko on its body, and it was a guardian to a sacred taonga (treasure) from one of our Tipuna (ancestors) that was in the lake. If it was seen, you were to take the green stone it was guarding as it is meant for you. My Koro said they didn't take it because they got scared, so they went back to shore on their boat. After hearing that story, I knew it was MY eel. The eel I dreamt about since I was seven years old. I told my dad about my dreams, and he nurtured my spiritual curiosity ever since.

Growing up I always felt a little different. I was shy as a child and seemed to come out of my shell in my teenage years. I was used to having dreams that meant something or had a message in them, and I knew which dreams needed attention. Every time I went outside of my tribal boundaries, I would have a dream. Usually they were friendly reminders that my ancestors were with me. During my teenage years I could see things that were from the spirit world. They would mainly manifest as mist or swirling smoke. The misty one was okay, but the smokey one was not. I got to learn very quickly what it felt like to have different energies come close to me, even touch me, and some were not nice at all.

My father is a big influence in my spiritual development and my transformational journey. He has always nurtured this insight that was developing within me. He was my dream de-coder and spirit cleanser. He taught me all about the strength of the creator and faith in belief to stay in the light, and all of this was done through our Maori culture, Taha Wairua (spiritual knowledge). Being Maori and spiritual is not an uncommon thing, so I was not seen as being different as you would in non-indigenous societies. These gifts were encouraged in our culture and nurtured. Those that possessed this gift were feared for having this knowledge, and our history tells of burdens to those that held Tohungaship (shamanism).

PART 1 - Leading From Within

Life continued and I had a family. I felt a pull to move to Australia and further develop my career as a teacher. My parents, sister, husband and three children at the time made the journey across the Tasman and settled in Melbourne. Quickly we settled in, and almost immediately my spiritual journey continued to shape and take form. I met a gorgeous bunch of women living here from New Zealand that introduced me to a spiritual teacher living in Rosebud. She was the first teacher who taught me how to meditate. This was when my dreams could communicate with me on a conscious level.

Meditating scared me at first, not because of the unknown but because I felt I was betraying my culture and my indigeneity. I was learning about other divine gods and beings, when all I knew were the gods of my culture. My ancestors and creatures were my guides. One of my early meditations put this feeling of betrayal to rest. In this meditation, which I will never forget, I saw a pathway. I walked along this pathway that was lined with Maori warriors dressed in full traditional dress. As I walked, these warriors flipped between being Maori and being white angels. I finally understood what this divine message was about. We are all the same, every creed, every race. We are from the same energy, the same divine light.

This is when my spiritual world opened up to the wonders of other cosmic knowledge. I was tuned into the spirit world of my ancestors and began receiving messages from them about Taha Wairua (spiritual teachings). All of this was being received while I was living in Melbourne, Australia.

I went through some significant self-transformations. My eel came back to me through meditation, and this time I could talk to him. From the bottom of the lake, he gave me a choice. I was given three things: a large green stone patu (weapon), bone (human) and feathers. These belonged to an ancestor and the story I was told tells of how his green stone was never found and the eel is the guardian. I chose to take these items. At the time I wasn't sure why, but felt I had to take these gifts. When I learnt what I could from the eel and my soul began to awaken more, my guide changed from an eel to a dragonfly. In meditation and dream I was able to fly across the countryside (NZ) and go to untouched peaceful places. My dragonfly took me to many guides who taught me how to feel when change is coming by watching the wind and the birds, how to see without eyes and how to heal. The freedom of the dragonfly is magical, and the opportunities he opens up for learning are liberating.

I was taken on a special journey, and I had only recognised how significant this journey was when I had a coaching day with one of my business mentors. My transformational journey came from the moment of transition from eel to the dragonfly. The eel cannot leave his waterways, and he is always in the same place and at times stagnant. The eel gave me the choice to take the gifts I needed in the world or remain here in the same place. Unbeknown at the time, I chose freedom and liberation. That is when the dragonfly came for me. I still had no idea what the gifts from the eel meant until now, 12 years later!

These are gifts I needed to be The Soulful Leader and to lead others on their way to being soulful leaders too. These three things represent the lifeblood, the three core elements to being a soulful leader, which I will share with you later in this book. The greenstone is the spirit and heart, the feathers are the insight and values and the bone is the impulse and movement. These are the gifts that belonged to a great warrior chief from my tribe, and they were gifted to me esoterically to give to other great soulful warriors of our time. Leadership is more than a responsibility: it is a gift, a gift that can transform your life from the stagnant murky waters to the fresh winds of the tide. You have the choice to take these gifts and free yourself, and you don't have to wait 12 years to understand what it all means.

The Soulful Transition and The Crossroad

The point of my soulful journey is to help you find yours and, most importantly, identify the soulful transition that is significant in your soulful leadership development. If we do not fully understand the transition that has blessed our journey, then we cannot fully grasp the true meaning of the task at hand or the expansiveness of our mission or purpose. The transition is a checkpoint of spiritual and personal growth. It is the turning point or the realisation that you have chosen a particular path, whether you are conscious of it or not.

It took me years to unpack my soulful transition and the symbolic meaning behind it. The reason it took years was I needed the experiences to gain readiness and spiritual maturity to understand its grand meaning. Even though I experienced this transition 12 years ago, the transition at that time had a different meaning. It was the introduction of my spiritual path, and now I understand it was more than introductions, more like an initiation or test for accepting the knowledge that I promised I would share with those willing to listen and learn. The beauty about connecting with the grand meaning of your transitions is it will bring you to your crossroad. Your crossroad may not be apparent at first, but over a timeline of soulful transitions and specific soulful awakenings, you will find yourself standing at a clear intersection that makes your heart sing.

The crossroad or the intersection in life is not the fork in the road you come to and choices need to be made, but rather the purposeful path you have chosen and why you stand by it. Steve Jobs understood his creative purpose and stood at the crossroad of "Technology and Liberal Arts." Everything he created was from the crossroad of his purpose to create: "Technology is not enough... It's technology married with liberal arts, married with humanities, that yields us the result that make our hearts sing." (Steve Jobs, 2011 iPad2 launch).

It takes a lot of clarifying and soul journeys to narrow in on a clear crossroad, but it is there and it is at the point of your soulful transition. I understood the power of standing at my crossroad when I grasped my purpose and married my entrepreneurial journey (Kid Coach) together, creating my point of position in all I do at the crossroads of "Personal Development and Liberal Educational." Since this crossroad, I have had another personal awakening that has lead me to stand at another junction (The Soulful Leader) of "Personal Development and Leadership."

Identifying Your Soulful Transition

Identifying your soulful transition is not easy, and it will take some deep soul searching and personal development before you can truly identify, resonate and reflect on the point of your soulful transition. You can have many soulful transitions as our spiritual growth and soul evolution will go through many levels of awareness. Here is a question that you could ask yourself to help identify the transition points quicker and allow the reflection to begin as your soulful journey unfolds.

Identifying Your Soulful Transitions

Exercise #2

What significant events have occurred in your life that have had a heartfelt, drop into reality or spirit feeling for you? Write down as many as you can remember. When you have written them all down, place them on a timeline of chronological order. You should notice a developmental pattern of your soul's journey.

These events are usually spiritual in feeling so they may occur during a retreat, workshop, healing and meditation, being in nature, deep thought or even despair.

_____

_____

_____

PART 1 - Leading From Within

A friend of mine shared her amazing soulful transition story with me.

"I thought the house in the country and my job was the perfect life that I had dreamed of. So why was everything turning out to be the opposite of what I had hoped? I remember driving in my car feeling down, frustrated and confused about where I was heading in life. I pulled the car over so I could cry out my hurt and frustration. I got out of the car and walked to the grass on the side of the road, in my heart asking for help and guidance. Like an answered prayer, a beautiful beam of light shone through the grey sky right down by my feet where a beautiful bright red spotted toadstool was. Right at that moment I felt as if my prayers had been answered and I knew what I was here to do. I cried and cried, not out of frustration and confusion anymore, but from an awakened moment that connected with my inner being. I found my calling, my purpose."

For my friend, seeing the sunlight beaming onto the beautiful toadstool was the physical identity of her soulful transition and the spiritual identity was the emotional sense of feeling clarity in her future direction and feeling supported. Her significant moment helped her pinpoint her next action point with her life and family as well as her purpose as a soulful leader. She is an advocate for children's wellbeing through helping parents parent from a mindful perspective.

PART 2

The Shift

Chapter 3: Earth's Evolution

"The most powerful weapon on Earth is the human soul on fire."
-Ferdinand Foch

You might be wondering what does the earth have to do with leadership? According to native wisdom and ancient perspectives on leadership being related to life on Earth, it is the very core fabric of soulful leadership. Earth's evolution is important to our role as soulful leaders on this planet. We are connected to this planet as it sustains and nurtures life for every human (something we seem to have swayed from in modern times). Earth's energy is abundant in life sustaining resources and creativity.

As the earth develops and changes over time, so do human beings, and this is evident in our history. It is also evident in our leadership capacity. We are developing and evolving with the earth. Our souls and the earth are aligned, and ancient indigenous people knew this.

Going with the ancient perspective on leadership being life and life being the sustainability of our earth and human survival, it is a no brainer that the earth has everything to do with our capacity to lead as a soulful leader. I'm not talking about being a hippie radical leader (although there is nothing wrong with that), but I'm talking about the deeper understanding of our place on this planet and a deeper understanding of the type of leaders this world needs. The soulful leaders of today are aligned with the earth's energy and her evolution. Soulful leaders have evolved into consciously aware humans and are connected to Earth's beauty, aliveness, wonder, adventure, creativeness and so much more. A lot more businesses with soulful leaders are giving back to organisations that make a difference to the planet or to people in need of support. We are seeing a rise in social and environmental awareness and global connection has a lot to do with this awareness.

A Global Awakening

We are not just villagers anymore, only having access to neighbours or close towns. We are a global community. Technology has given us the gift of global connection. With the invention of the Internet, we have been able to see that we are not alone in our feelings and in our callings. When I got clarity on my calling to awaken soulful leaders, I saw a book written by Japp Geerlof called *The Awakening of the Soulful Leaders*. The universe of course, put this in front of me many times and even sent me an email that eventually I bought it.

I had only looked at the contents of the book and realised that we have definitely tapped into the same source to gather this information, and the divine messages of being a collective conscious is accurate. He has written his book in his mother tongue, but I am lucky that it has been translated into English. My point to this is there is a divine message on a global scale to awaken soulful leaders. Even soulful leaders that do not speak the same language can have the same collective vision. That is friggen awesome!

Global-ness...(divine message)

Global is a human explanation to bring each other together. In the bigger version of things we are not apart at all. Physical environments separate us, but the heart song stays intact. It is when we start to speak the same soul language that we find each other again and can connect to that awakening.

I know I'm not alone in this movement and I am an advocate and leader for this global awakening. There are more people in this movement, and I have been told by divine guidance that it is more than just an awakening of leaders in a professional position, but of those that hold the positions of love and peace in the household. Soulful leadership is about living and loving life to its full capacity. Your work becomes part of your life where it has a greater purpose to serve others to lift them to a better place. If your work is a full time housewife or husband, then your soulful leadership is to serve yourself in a way that is for the greater good of your family.

Knowing when to nourish your soul is essential to loving and nourishing those around you. If we do not find time to nourish the soul, we become agitated, shitty and even angry. The worst thing is this ugly energy starts to spew across to others and in other areas of our lives and it turns to bitterness and the "Oh, woe is me" syndrome. This syndrome is a broken record mantra that I dislike hearing. It screeches blame, no responsibility and more blame.

When you are awake, your record (the screechy one) will not play the same way. Your music will change and you will listen to reflective notes where you begin to see why certain things did not happen for you before and where you want to be. This is when the heart song and soul language play in unison and it's an awesome tune. This is the tune that awakens every cell in your body to something greater. Your cells burst into a rejuvenated youthful essence and you want to make changes for a better you and a better life. This is the awakening.

Awakening...

The awakening has been a gradual process. This is timed perfectly in line with universal development. Each planet and star is in a process of development and awakening and rejuvenation. We are no different to planets, stars and living things. We have a process. Your process will *depend on where your cosmic evolutionary life is. Our lives are on an evolutionary path that is foreseen. You have seen this and you are the creator of awakenings and lessons. Before you step here into the earthly realm, you have made your soul song with your higher self and you will play your song until your earthly self can hear it and then you know it is time. Your soul song will never stop. It is a direct path to divine guidance.*

Global Shift

Technology has given us the ability to become globally connected. We can connect with groups and networks through social media and share our views with someone across the globe. We can also travel these distances with ease. Making decisions to move to another country is made easy with air, sea and wireless technology. This world is damn amazing and we don't take the time to appreciate it enough.

The global shift I want to mention is how we are becoming connected as a collective. You may have heard this before: "We are all ONE." I heard it many times, but did not fathom its greater relevance. In a divine message, which I will share with you shortly, I finally understood "We are all ONE." When we are shifting, we are shifting our energies in alignment with each other. When we are aligned, the technology helps us connect on a face-to-face basis, but it is all about the conscious energy shift first.

We are making these shifts because of the awakening the earth is going through. According to the Mayan calendar, the 13th Baktun ended in 2012 and on the 22nd December 2012, a new cycle began. This is the earth's evolutionary cycle too and as she ascends, so do our energetic vibrations. We are able to connect and hear our soul songs more easily than before. It doesn't take as much discipline and forced focus and concentration to be able to connect with divine guidance. We are shifting more into our bodies so we can connect with our senses to experience sensations again.

This dual ascension (planetary and human) has shifted a lot of energy and cleared way for new and exciting times. With the combination of universal knowledge and technology we were all able to help the earth's energy hold as much light energy for our vibrations to rise in unison. This is the greatest gift of technology and the timing of its existence is perfect. I remember watching Mayan elder talks on You Tube and participating in the first sun dances in my back yard to harness as much energy for the earth's evolution as I could, along with millions of others around the globe. Having the ability to contribute and participate in worldly events is much easier with the help of multi-media.

We are shifting into a new world.

The Collective Consciousness

This is the true reason for the global shift. We are tapping into the source of the collective.

What is the source of the collective?

Well it is the everlasting energy source, light of God, white light, whatever you want to call it. It is a huge pool of energy that we all have access to. I like to refer to this source as the life force purely because it is the essence of life and our existence. I guess this pool could be described as the fountain of youth: it never runs dry and any one can drink from it. The only thing is the fountain can be a journey to get to and the journey is always your own personal self-development and transformation. Your transformation, your awakening is the key to the fountain of youth or your life force.

PART 2 - The Shift

As I was saying, we are all part of the collective because we all drink from the same fountain, if you want to, some choose not to and will eventually, in their own time. Because we are drinking from the same source, we are connected in the same energetic essence that we nourish ourselves with when we drink. We are all the same energy, the same life force. The collective that choose to tap into this pool are awakened to the world's consciousness. They are and will be the new worlds, leaders, the new world's entrepreneurs, the new world's parents, and live loving and fulfilling lives. Sounds a little bit like a preachy promised land scripture, I know, but it is a new world consciousness.

The conscious pool helps the earth and human beings to raise their energetic vibrations. When we use this source vibrations, our energy levels rise higher. This vibration allows us to consciously connect to a higher guidance. Quite simply, the more we use the life force, the more compassionate and loving we become. We start to think more on a collective level rather than for ourselves on an egotistical level. We make choices that benefit a greater good and nourish the soul. We listen deeply to our heart song and we act in accordance to the tune.

I was taught the source that we all tap into by my spiritual teachers years ago, but I did not fully take it into my awareness until the time was right for me to move my business into the field of awakening soulful leaders. Now I understand the importance and the full capacity of using the fountain of youth or life force. This is what we are missing in our lives and our leadership. If we tapped into the collective conscious pool, we would be very different leaders, and I'm not talking the woo-woo stuff. I'm talking about being wise beyond your years, speaking from a place of truth and heart and actions that define integrity and soul. There is nothing more awe-inspiring, captivating and just damn awesome than a leader that comes from this space. The Soulful Leader is all about leading from this space.

I want to share a divine message I received when I was getting clear on my business vision...and a damn clear vision it was too. This message clearly describes the purpose of the conscious pool and soul communication. You may not understand it at first...I didn't, but it will land when you are ready for it. Every time I read it, I get another a-ha moment.

The vision for The Soulful Leader...(divine message)

Do the things that make your heart sing, melt, and soar.

You are a divine being with an ultimate divine message.

You have heard us. You listened to your heart and we will listen to yours.

We are all one conscious soul acting out many conscious creations, some light, some dark, but they are all part of the conscious pool and it is all balanced.

...

Understanding that every dark creation and light is a soul balance is hard for human consciousness to grasp, and for that we love them.

We love their passion and drive and that is where your purpose lies.

You are to harness that passion and drive and help them create more light for the conscious pool.

This will help the universe raise its collective vibration.

The vibration is a frequency that is needed to connect everyone together.

It is our soul communication. The collective.

PART 2 - The Shift

Why do we need soul communication?

Human consciousness and design does not understand this system of communication.

They are too worried about dark thoughts and secrets.

Soul communication is more than thoughts; it is a whole and total being.

In soul communication no one has ill thoughts or feelings.

We feel it all: the love, joy and pain.

It is not comprehendible to human consciousness, but it can be experienced.

This is true peace and love. There is no harm or hurt.

Chapter 4:
Aligning With The Collective Consciousness

*"Cut not the wings of your dreams,
for they are the heartbeat and the freedom of your soul."*
-Flavia

Soulful leaders are finding they want to align themselves to the collective consciousness because of the earth's evolution. There is a massive and quite radical shift in the earth's vibrational energy. This radical shift is in the hearts and minds of the people living on earth, us! Every 13,000 years, the earth's energy (Kundalini) moves, leading us into a higher spiritual vibration. The Kundalini is attached to the hearts of humankind, and as Earth evolves herself, so do we. We are awakening to something far greater than our own personal gratification. It is a far greater awakening of love and peace, even among the war and devastation we see in the media. We want love, harmony and peace in our lives. We want more love in our intimate and non-intimate relationships. We are searching for peace in our hearts and harmony in our environments because of our connection to this global phenomenon. And it all begins through an opening to the soul.

Opening the Soul

Your soul is on a vibrational level where it can begin to communicate better with you due to the energy shift of the earth's evolution. Some have always been able to communicate soulfully, and others have found this a hard thing to do. Your soul has always spoken to you as the divine message told us in the calling...*help is in many forms. Forms of beauty, musical, peaceful and connected moments...*these are the communications of the soul. How beautiful to think that your soul speaks to you through your senses. In essence, that is exactly how your soul speaks to you.

Along the way we have become so de-sensitised from our bodies and emotions that we cut off our soulfulness. When we are soulless, we are numb to touch, taste, hearing, sight and smell. This is the zombie apocalypse taking over the world, soulless senseless beings walking around this earth not experiencing anything! At least there is a cure, and it's called "soul connection." This makes me laugh; my teenage daughters love zombie movies, and they would roll their eyes if they read the above and tell me it's not exciting enough.

Opening the soul is about the simplicity and miracle of our senses.

Why your senses... (divine message)

God gave us this form of communication so that you may always talk to him directly whenever you need him. It worked perfectly for a long time. until other energies took over and we forgot how to communicate this way. We have been waiting for this to re-open to begin communicating again and to re-energise your bodies. Your bodies are a gift that is especially designed to feel, taste, smell, hear, touch and, most of all, create. They are designed for the density of Earth, and Earth is the only place where you can feel all these things so intensely. It is the sensory planet where all lessons are really accounted for and learned.

Nowhere in this universe can we feel the way we do when learning as we do on Earth. Your earthly experiences are for a greater purpose. Each time we go through a learning life, we help someone else work through there own purposes and lessons. The opening to this will help everyone work through pain with less pain and love with more love. Sensory awareness is the key to feel it all and honour it as it stands. When we honour every feeling, we are grateful for what it teaches us. This brings attention to the temple in which houses sensory acuity, your bodies. It is more important than ever to take care of your body, to experience each sense with gratitude and ease.

The Key To Your Soul

Your soul loves sensations, all of them, the good and the unpleasant. Senses are a great way for humans to get back into feeling what's going on in the body. With so much outward sensory stimulation in our modern world, we have almost become numb and desensitised from the sensations and feelings within our body. It's like a drug; the sensation lasts for a moment and then we are after the next fix. We have lost the art of holding the pleasure of our senses within our bodies and stimulating pathways to the soul. Your soul is alive when it can experience things that are in real time and in the moment. True sensory acuity is experienced in the present moment.

This awakens a communication pathway with your soul, enlivens your senses and surges a movement of energy within your body. This is where mindful practices are fabulous. Mindful practices help us to experience a connection with things in the present moment. Mindfulness is the practice of being present in the moment and being aware of your connection to things around you. This could be the moments you are spending with your children, family, friends or work. The awareness is when you are connected to your surroundings through a sensory experience or a learning sensation.

To awaken the pathway of communication to your soul, I have included 13 sensory exercises for you to practise. An exercise each day for one of your senses is a fantastic sensual place to begin enlivening your soul and connecting more with your body. In your diary or journal, write down a sense and do one of the mindful practices to get your senses buzzing. Remember, even an unpleasant sensory experience is still a sensory awakening. Embrace all of your sensings the good and the unpleasant. Bring each of these feelings into your body and notice how it feels when you bring each sense within you and hold it for as long as you can.

Soul Sensory

Touch

Exercise #1

Feel you arm with your fingertips. Slowly caress your arm with your fingertips. Notice how your skin feels. Notice everything about your touch. Give thanks and gratitude for being able to touch and feel these sensations. You can do this practise with another part of your body, like your hands, feet, face etc.

___

___

___

Exercise #2

Massage. This can be done with an intimate partner. With your partner, slowly feel their neck. Notice how their skin feels and how you feel when you touch them. Feel across their shoulder and down their arms. Be absolutely present with every touch. Work over your partner's body, and most importantly, notice all your sensations when you touch them. Give thanks and gratitude for the gift of sensual touch to this beautiful person.

___

___

___

Exercise #3

Object of touch. Whatever you have in your hand, go into the sensation of feeling its exterior. Feel it with your fingertips. Notice how the surface feels and the temperature of it. Give thanks and gratitude for the sense of touch and the purpose the object has in making your life more beautiful.

_____

_____

_____

Hear

Exercise #4

Nature sounds. For 2-5 minutes, give yourself the gift of nature's peaceful sounds. Just sit and listen to the ocean, or birds or anywhere you can be peaceful. If you cannot find an open space to be at peace, then listen to a nature sound CD. Notice how these sounds make your body feel. Give thanks and gratitude for the sense of hearing and the amazing gift of nature's sounds that bring us peace and calm.

_____

_____

_____

PART 2 - The Shift

Exercise #5

Listen. Listen to someone so intently without need to make a comment. Listen to this person with your eyes. Notice how your undivided attention makes them feel valued and loved. Notice how listening to them allows you to understand them more deeply. You can do this one with your partner and notice how deep your understanding of them becomes. Give thanks and gratitude for the sense of hearing and listening to understand others more deeply.

_____

_____

_____

Exercise #6

Café ears. Sit in a café and just listen to the conversations that are happening around you. Just listen with open ears. Notice how people laugh, how they whisper intently or how they speak louder with excitement. Give thanks and gratitude for the sense of hearing and the conversations that we can have with others to express a variation of emotions.

_____

_____

_____

Smell

Exercise #7

Love food. When you do your shopping, especially raw fruits and vegetables, take a moment to smell them. Notice the freshness, the rawness, and the goodness. Notice how your body tingles or sings with the smell of good food. Give thanks and gratitude for the sense of smell and the abundance of good food for our body.

_____

_____

_____

Exercise #8

Cooking. When you cook your meal or have it cooked for you, take a moment to smell the love that has gone into this cooked meal. Notice the sauces or herbs. Smell the nourishment in this meal. Give thanks and gratitude for the sense of smell and the love that went into the meal that feeds and nourishes your body.

_____

_____

_____

PART 2 - The Shift

Exercise #9

Perfume. You can find you a fragrance or flower that has a smell that you love. Surround yourself with this fragrance or wear it. Notice how this fragrance makes you feel. You may feel sensual, pleasurable, sexy or confident. Notice how your body shifts into your state of feeling e.g. sexy or confident. Give thanks and gratitude for the sense of smell and the way this fragrance makes you feel.

_____

_____

_____

Taste

Exercise #10

Soul food. Have a snack moment and get yourself some raw food or a piece of chocolate. We are going to combine a few senses here to make this more sensual and divine. First, feel your piece of soul food. Notice how it feels inside your body to touch its surface. Smell your piece of soul food. Notice how this sends tingles or song through your nerve endings.

Now place your soul food into your mouth if it's chocolate and let it sit on your tongue. Notice how your mouth starts to work. Tastebuds pop, saliva increases and you want to swallow the taste into your body. If you are biting your soul food, notice how your teeth feel when it they bite into the food. Notice where the food wants to go next and how your tongue pushes it to where it needs to go. Notice how your tastebuds pop with excitement. Feel the nourishment of the soul food enlivening your cells as you swallow. Give thanks and gratitude to the sensual sense of taste and the wonders of our mouths to know what to do.

Exercise #11

Eating. Any meals you eat begin with being mindful of its taste. The sense of taste is so sensual and every meal should be a sensual experience in the way it makes your body and soul sing. Remember this when you eat and always give thanks and gratitude for the food we eat.

Sight

Exercise #12

This sense is the gift of beauty. Surround yourself with beauty. Pick fresh flowers from the garden or buy them to brighten up your environment. You may like to use crystals or candles. Notice how seeing beauty around you makes you feel. Give thanks and gratitude for the sense of sight and the wonder of beauty.

PART 2 - The Shift

Exercise #13

I see you. When you are with your partner or a friend, see them deeply. Not the outside appearance, but "see" what they say to you when they talk. "See" how they act to you when they are around. "See" how they treat others and talk about them. Give thanks and gratitude for this person in helping you see things more clearly and deeply.

_____

_____

_____

PART 3
Native Wisdom of Leadership

Chapter 5:
Native Wisdom of Life

"Naku te rourou nau te rourou ka ora ai te iwi."
(With your basket and my basket the people will live)
Maori Proverb

Native wisdom of life is based on every living thing possessing the "life force." The life force is the gift Great Spirit gave to all things through the creation process. Leadership is how we utilise our life force to do greater good on Earth. Leadership is a far greater responsibility than just a role you play in your everyday job. True leadership, soulful leadership is concerned with the role your life force plays on a greater scale that awakens all those within your influence to participate and contribute with the highest morals and cultural virtues as gifted by Great Spirit.

Native wisdom describes the life force as the three core elements that will be explained in chapters 6-8 and is the essence soulful leaders possess. This is a powerful concept in leadership development, and I have seen nothing out there that comes close to this. Equipping leaders with native wisdom is worth more than a Masters Degree in Leadership. Native wisdom is the life force of soulful leaders and has the capacity to help anyone create and love the life they are meant to lead. It has the capacity to help you think and dream big, for it comes from a deep soul space that we don't often take the time to listen to. Our world is fast and noisy, and we have a hard time going inward to hear what our soul is saying to us.

PART 3 - Native Wisdom of Leadership

Listen...(divine message)

Going inward can connect you to your soul. Your soul has a divine message for you and it wants to sing to you. Allow yourself time to stop and look at the beauty that surrounds you. You will be surprised at the voice you may hear singing back to you. Make time for quiet listening. Make time to listen to your family and friends. You will hear your soul through them too. Just listen.

Native wisdom is the simplest tool of leadership-development, and it is the same architectural design told through my culture's knowledge about the creation of the universe. What I am about to share with you is a gift that is as old as the beginning of our universe. The life force is what created the big bang, and it will create the same concept in re-birthing your leadership. To understand this concept, you will need to understand its origins and have appreciation and gratitude for being part of the great circle that is creation...life.

I want to share a native narrative told to me through my cultures understanding of our connection to the life force. These stories were only given to those in the tribe that held status and divine understanding, usually a tohunga (shaman) or Matakite (seer). Now that you are awakened, you will understand the divine wisdom in this story.

Native Narrative – The Creation Story

In the beginning there was a vast ocean of nothingness. The nothingness (Te Kore) spanned endless space and endless time. Great Spirit (Io) the supreme god resided in the nothingness. He remained unseen in the depths of emptiness and forever eternal. Stirring from his deep slumber, Great Spirit yearned to love.

Great Spirit set to work in creating his grandest plan. His plan required careful and precise mastery. From the depths of nothingness, Great Spirit could see beauty in her emptiness. Nothingness had many qualities, which were birthed as her children. Her children are The Great Nothingness, The Long Nothingness, The Nothingness of the Seer, The Intangible Nothingness, The Excited Nothingness and the Boundless Nothingness.

All though the nothingness had many children, she felt lonely. Great Spirit felt her loneliness and sent her a partner to embrace her and hold her close. The Darkness (Te Po) and The nothingness (Te Kore) had an everlasting embrace, which formed the womb of creation. In this union of Nothingness and Darkness, many children were birthed, The Everlasting Darkness, The Long Darkness, The Intense Darkness, The Great Darkness, The Extreme Darkness, The Absorbing Darkness and The Complete Darkness. The Nothingness and the Darkness embrace and embody love and everlasting, for there to be light, there must be darkness.

The Nothingness and the eternal embrace of The Darkness and their children remained the same. There was no yesterday, tomorrow, no past, no future and the nothingness began to stir with restlessness. Great Spirit felt the unease and stirring of her restlessness and gifted them both a child. An immaculate child with the gift of Time that immediately gave birth to a child with the gift of Change.

Time now created the opportunity for things to be done and for a moment to be. The Nothingness could be present in the now with the eternal embrace of Darkness and watch adoringly as her children created the birth of life, becoming the prime laws of the universe. Time and Change have created purposefulness. The purposefulness of the "now" and experiencing "being present" and the purposefulness of "becoming" and experiencing change.

With wonder and possibility gifted to the universe through the birth of Time and Change, expansive and vast energy created change in each child of the darkness. The being and becoming interactive change of each child created the universe as we know it. And our universe is still vast and expansive and ever-changing.

Great Spirit loved the excitement of change and interaction but found his architecture without structure, so he gifted the prime laws (Time and Change) the essence of Spirit (Mana). Spirit stood timeless, complete and whole. Spirit is full of truth, integrity and justice and hearing the word of Great Spirit in his ethics, values and beliefs. Spirit is the gift of unconditional love, for Time and Change are birthed in the image of Great Spirit himself.

Time and Change loved the gift of Spirit, but found Spirit was rigid and remained still in truth and justice. So Great Spirit sent another gift, the essence of Impulse (Mauri). He sent Impulse to allow Spirit to surge and flow his essence across the Darkness. Impulse is movement and energy, the life force that turns, twists and shapes. Impulse is excitement, passion and purpose.

Now Time and Change possessed two gifts: the essence of Spirit and Impulse given to them out of pure love from Great Spirit, but Great Spirit with his architectural foresight could see they needed to possess one more essence to bring his great plan to light. So with love he gifted Time and Change the essence of Design (Maui). Design is balance and harmony. Great Spirit gave Time and Change his last gift of supreme understanding and survival. Design is elegance and flow, rhythm and tide. It is the wonderful cycle of renewal and connection to all things.

Great Spirit was pleased with his grand plan and loved the different facets of all his children. He loved their sporadic movement and curious exploration. Seeing how each child wondered far and wide, Great Spirit became worried that his children may stray and get lost, not finding their way back. So he gave the gift of the Two Waters (Wairua). He gave the Two Waters to the Nothingness and the Darkness in the form of the universal womb and asked them to keep Two Waters as the gateway for the children's return if they should ever stray. The Two Waters worked in miraculous ways to birth creativity and share it with Great Spirit.

Great Spirit's divine architecture of pure love and creativity is the source and DNA of all living things. Great Spirit created all living things in the divine image of himself, pure and unconditional love.

The Essence of Creation

The creation story or dreamtime story holds the essence of life. It holds all the knowledge we need to manifest our greatest dreams in our lifetime. This is an ancient knowledge born from the beginning of time and has been forgotten due to our human thirst for power and ego. More people in the world have been unlocking the purpose of life and the key to living it through indigenous and ancient stories. It is my intention to unlock the key to soulful leadership through the native wisdom and ancient knowledge as I know it and as it has been given to me to share with you. We are creative beings, born from creativity and destined to live by creativity for it is divine universal law that tells us so. Put this into the context of your own life, job or business.

> Are you using creativity in your life?
> Are you creating the things that you desire?

Everything told through my culture's ancient native wisdom always had a union or whakapapa (genealogy). The union is of the masculine and feminine essence. This becomes the bases for creativity. Within creativity are certain primal laws and core elements. The primal laws of time and change have different meaning. Let me try to explain the complexity of time and change in a spiritual and earthly concept. In the spiritual realm, time has no concept, yet it needs to exist in order to birth or create change. On our earthly plane, time exists to manage aspects of life. Moon cycles and seasons are concepts of Earth time, while time zones are human concepts. Each concept is important for getting things done and making change occur.

The true concept of time is that it doesn't exist, but only in the moment or in being. Everything happens in the moment and in that moment, time stands still and change occurs before your eyes. In that present moment, you are able to understand the time before the change occurs and what the future time may hold. The primal law of time and change only exists in the present moment or the realisation of being.

I understand that the concept of time is hard to comprehend; it has taken years for this to click with me, and I only fully understood the concept when I researched further into my culture's creation stories. Many spiritual people and teachers have spoken of time not being relevant or not existing. I could understand it in spiritual terms, but it was difficult to understand on this earthly plane when everything we do has a cyclic, seasonal or time zone attached to our daily lives. We need each of our earthly and human time concepts to manage a way of life, but there is a deeper meaning and relevance to the existence time has in the two worlds (spiritual and earthly).

In the present moment is when these two worlds meet. This meeting of worlds happens in the event that is occurring around you. You become connected to this event through deep emotional awareness. In this moment of being, or "being present," you have brought these two worlds into alignment. So time and change become the gateway of the two worlds meeting, as Time and Change are primal laws of the "present moment of being."

When this gateway is open and you are in the state of being or being present, this is when the three core elements come into play. The three core elements are the gifts that Great Spirit (Io) gave to the primal laws, Time and Change, to give them structure, stability and survival.

The first element is Spirit (Mana), holding virtues of love, truth, integrity, justice and divine ethics and beliefs. The Spirit element has a feminine energy and resides in the heart or heart chakra of our bodies.

The second element is Impulse (Mauri). The Impulse is energy and movement. It is the life force and energy of our purpose and passion. The Impulse is the union and has both feminine and masculine energy and resides 2-3 inches below the navel or the sacral chakra.

The third element is Insight (Maui), holding virtues of harmony and balance. Insight has a pure understanding of survival and the cycle of life and our connectedness to it. Insight is masculine in energy and resides in the pineal gland or third eye chakra.

Great Spirit, being the supreme architect of the universe, came to a time where he created man. He created man in the light of himself, which are the three core elements he gifted to Time and Change. Because his creation was perfect, time and time again he used the same creation concept when creating the first man and the first woman. Each human was given the gift of Spirit, Impulse and Insight to do great things on Earth. The soul of each man and woman is made up of all three elements. That is why I call them the three core elements. They are core to anything else and when connected, become the soul essence. Separately, the three elements give us great insight in our lives and leadership, but together they make for powerful transformation, understanding and enlightenment.

PART 4

Te Mana

Chapter 6:
Spirit – The Feminine

"When you feel you are being moved by the creative spirit, you are in fact being moved by the divine feminine."
Teri Degler

I just looked up the meaning of Mana in the online maoridictionary.co.nz, and it interested me that the definition read, *"mana is a supernatural force in a person, place or object."* Growing up as a young Maori girl, I always new that someone who had Mana, was someone high up, like a chief, kaumatua (respected elder) or an authority figure. I love how the dictionary adds a supernatural force because that's exactly the best way to explain all these elements. We would also say spirit is a supernatural force so even though Spirit and Mana have different meanings in my culture, the essence is still the same.

The other concept around Mana is it has a very masculine connotation. In my culture, men have the Mana on a Marae (traditional meeting house), where men only may stand and speak to visitors. In some tribal areas this is different, so I am talking from Te Arawa decent and background.

To fully grasp Spirit and Mana as it is universally intended, I had to open my eyes and heart to the world and other cultures. This sent me on a journey to Australia with my family. Not that I knew this was a spiritual journey, but it became quickly apparent when the first people we met in Australia were Maori whanau (NZ extended family) that were in a meditation group and invited my mother and I along. The journey to universal spirituality began. I call this universal because all my life I was bought up very spiritual but through a cultural perspective, which can be likened to being strictly bought up in a religion.

PART 4 - Te Mana

I love my culture and the identity I proudly align with. I love our rich history, narratives, native wisdom and bloodlines. What I love most is the yearning to keep pure the history and stories alive for our youth. Like any religion, my culture is based on fear of the unknown and the unseen. Breaking out of my comfort zone and fear orientation of the dos and don'ts of my culture, I was able to break down the veil over my eyes and open them to the option that I am part of Great Spirit (Io) through the gift of Mana - Spirit. So I wanted to explore the full extent of this element.

The Gift

Spirit is the feminine essence that resides in the heart in our body and both men and women need this feminine element. Being in feminine essence does not mean being girly, it means using the essence of feminine energies such as being heart-orientated, intuitive, creative, trusting, visualisation and receiving, just to name a few. This element has the capacity to expand the heart chakra to be open to receiving. Spirit is deeply entrenched in justice and integrity. Spirit allows us to be the divine priest or priestess to situations that require a balanced outcome without ego and fear and relies on intuition and trust. Spirit offers the true gift of unconditional love.

Spirit...(divine message)

Spirit is your personal judge and jury. Your serenity lies in your personal truth and not what you portray to others or the mask that you wear when you leave the comfort of your home. Spirit is the intuition to know when to stand for something and speak your truth. The world needs truth and Spirit needs to be set free. Spirit will be your beacon when you set sail on the vast sea of life. Spirit will always guide you and be a soothing song in your heart. Honour her, listen to her and act upon her request. She only works in your best interest.

Unconditional love isn't always easy and if it was, I bet the divorce rate wouldn't be so high. We are all born with these essences, and you see them so clearly in children. Children have the most potent form of unconditional love I have ever seen on this planet. A child will love their mother or father no matter how good or bad the situation they are born into. We would say they know no better, but you still can't deny that children hold and display Spirit in its purest form. When we forget how to love unconditionally, and it does happen, look to a young child to remind you how to love without wanting something in exchange or manipulating someone to get what you want.

The Virtues

Virtues are a way to help man live in harmony and balance. Without these virtues, man will not know how to harness the gift of Spirit. These virtues act as morals to guide each of us on an enlightened path.

Spirit's virtues are truth, justice and integrity. These morals are derived from Great Spirit's primary virtues that he gifted to all living things. These virtues have a different meaning and action when coupled with the gift of Spirit. We can see truth and justice in many different coloured lenses when we are not in tune to love. These coloured lenses are due to the environment and behaviours that we are born to and brought up in. Environmental conditions play a big role in the way we see and experience truth. Truth is a form of your own belief systems and what you were taught to believe. You are born into your family or culture's belief systems. These can be liberating or limiting beliefs depending on your family, culture or environment.

In my experience, culture can limit your beliefs, especially if there has been injustice or grievance within a culture. Fear and stereotyping is rampant when beliefs are limited. An extension to truth in a pro-active form is Justice. Most times, when a group of people believe that their truth is right and everyone else is wrong and they take an action of justice into a public forum, it is never done with love, let alone unconditional love. This is where acting with integrity is crucial. Integrity is the virtue that binds truth and justice with love.

Universal Intention

Each essence is given a universal intention and it is up to our own free will if we choose to accept it or create our own path. With the essence of Spirit, the universal intention is that of pure truth and unconditional love to deepen relationships with all living beings. To see others, truth and honour their truth without judgement is unconditional love in its purest form. Great Spirit's grand scheme was that all living things understand the true relationship to each other and honour it. The cycle of life is a true relationship of connectedness.

The intention is pretty plain and simple, as are all these essences and gifts. All one needs to do to be in the universal flow is to honour themselves with integrity. Be your own justifier and live by your truth. Allow others to live their truth and you remain integral to yours. You are the God of your own universe. Your relationship to others is to honour the many varieties of truth each person you meet will have. Each truth makes up the colours of the rainbow or the melting pot of the world. It is not by colour, race or creed that we should look at each other, but by the truth we present with and how creatively we live it. If we looked through the lens of universal intention of Spirit, your love for this world and the people in it would increase x10.

I am reminded of unconditional love in the eyes of my three-year-old. How cruel that our world unlearns this gift as soon as they are part of society or even in a family situation. I have been guilty of putting conditions on my children and aiding in the unlearning of unconditional love. I knew no better with my older children, and now that I had another chance to put my practise into training, I am much more aware of putting conditions on my children.

Do not get confused with conditions or expectations or use expectations as an excuse for using conditions. Conditions are when you expect something to be completed for approval. An expectation is an assumption that something will be done, like chores to be completed or homework to be done. As a teacher, I notice how so many children come to school with the behaviour of conditions on friendship. I'll be your friend if you give me this or if you do that and so on. I have heard parents call it bribery and find this a useful tool to get children to do what you want, but it is still putting on conditions for a particular outcome.

The problem comes when the condition is not met and the feeling of disappointment or being unloved is evident in a child. A parent may yell and rant, even take something away to prove their love has conditions. It is so unconscious, yet we do it all the time. The best way to get out of conditional and into unconditional is to offer a choice and then let your child engage in the outcome of whatever is chosen. Allowing someone to know that the choice is theirs and you will love him or her no matter what they choose, letting go of controlling the situation, is the key to unconditional love.

Real-World Intention

I've added real-world intentions to break down the grand scale of the universal intention to fit in with our everyday lives. I will admit that real-world intentions are always harder to do because we do make living so much more difficult than it was intended. In the real world, we need to have our own beliefs and values that align with Spirit. When we are younger, we are brought up with ideals and values, and as we experience

PART 4 - Te Mana

more of life, our belief systems may change depending on the experiences we are exposed to.

Real-world belief systems are that of the human psyche. They are the beliefs that we form in our heads or from our conditioning about people, places or how things should be done. They are not all necessarily true as they are contrived from a head space thought rather than a heart space feeling where Spirit resides. Real-world intentions are beliefs and values made from the space where Spirit resides. This is the true thought space of feeling rather than thought without the emotional experience. Most people can contrive a belief system by hearing someone else talk about it and not experience it for him or herself. How people perceive other races is a prime example of creating a belief system from the majority and not from personal experience. This is why the real-world intention is for everyone to experience the truth in life, whether it is good or bad, just experience things for you.

When we are exposed to our parent's family's or culture's beliefs, it becomes a part of who we are. Some of these beliefs we never question and most of the time we were not allowed to question them as that may have seemed disrespectful. A curious child may question beliefs, but is quickly shut down by parents or family members because they do not want their child to be different or fear what others may think. Yet it is curiosity that can break you free from limiting beliefs. Curiosity is the emotion that there could be more: more beauty, more wonder, more excitement. Curiosity is the thing that FEAR fears the most. Because just through the veil of fear is truth. Be curious enough to explore the things that you feel need questioning and allow children to explore their curiosity so they do not live in the fear of our beliefs.

My culture, just like religions is engulfed in fear. The true teachings are based on love, but man wanted to protect it so much that they created a barrier of fear around the precious teachings. Be good or this will happen, don't do that or this will happen was such a common thread in my culture and in other indigenous cultures too. It was put there to protect the spiritual nature of things, but as spirituality evolved, we forgot to evolve the teachings along with it. It should also be mentioned that indigenous cultures that were oppressed by colonisation were fearful of loosing their identity and taonga (treasure, gifts), which added to the fear of loosing their ancient knowledge and teachings. This fear gave the teachings a status where only the chosen or gifted would be presented with the ancient teachings. What I have noticed in the new light of our spiritual evolution is that the fear is releasing for many and more ancient knowledge is opening up to them.

My journey took me to Australia, where I opened up to the ancient teachings of my people. With a broken mother tongue (can't fluently speak my language), I was able to connect, understand and learn from my ancestors. I learnt the message is the same in any language, as our hearts are tuned into one language: the language of love. I became curious about all cultures and their connectedness to the spiritual world. I shifted drastically into a new awareness and followed this stream for years, being open to what comes through from the ancient and divine ones.

It was hard at first because I felt like I was betraying my culture. I was breaking through my conditioning. When I opened my heart, I was given the gift of truth. The truth about cultures, creeds and people of all walks of life and how we all fit into the grand scheme of the universe. There is not one single insignificant person on this planet.

Conditioning...(divine message)

Do not give in to the conditions that were dressed upon you. If the clothing does not fit right for you, then you have the right to change it. Be curious in your learning and stay open in your heart. Keep watch and listen and the truth will be revealed. We are all significant in the circle of life.

In and out of flow

When you are in the flow of Spirit and the virtues of Spirit, you will receive amazing life flow. This life flow is awesome if you are in business or leadership. Spirit offers a safe space to open your heart and see, hear and experience the truth of what it is you really want that is in the best interest of yourself or those you lead. Truth is absolute clarity in your endeavours. Spirit gives you the clarity you need to do what ever you seek out to do.

If you are in business or leadership, your clarity in decisions will come from opening your heart to the truth that is inside you. I guarantee your truth has manifested in the physical world at some time in your life to let you see and experience the joy of being in Spirit. Even if the truth is not what you wanted to see, hear or experience, it is however the clarity you need at that moment to make choices and decisions. With clarity also comes the ability to see what direction you are going in or want to go. You will see the path clearly and the small chunk-size goals it takes to get there. This is being IN the FLOW.

Being in the flow is great, but keeping yourself accountable to the direction you want to go in is the hardest thing to do. Having people or groups around you that can keep you accountable is key. Leaders who create teams help keep each other accountable to the organisational goals. Opening up to the guidance of Spirit will also help you to keep on task with your intentions.

When you are out of flow with Spirit, you will feel like you have no idea what you want, where you're going or what you are doing in your life, business or leadership. This is a horrible place to be and it's usually because your heart is closed off to your own truth. There are a few reasons why your heart is closed and the most common is because you feel unsafe to open up, usually because you have been hurt or ridiculed in the past. Out of flow is also our conditioning and when our beliefs are very limited due to upbringing or a lack of understanding or knowledge.

Limiting beliefs are detrimental to pure truth. There is no pure truth when your beliefs are limited. How can there be when you only see half of the story or person. This can make a person very rigid and unwilling to change, usually because they operate in fear and ego. They are afraid of the unknown and like to control their way through a limited belief system.

Out of flow journey...(divine message)

Those who are closed to Spirit need the soulful awakened ones to help them to open. They will open in time with lots of love and trust. This is also the gift of Spirit that is innate in the soulful ones. "Out of flow" is a journey, just as much on the truth and justice path as "In the flow." The path is the same, but the journeys are different.

Energy Work with Spirit

I have devised some practises that help evoke each of the essences. These practises will help open the heart to the song of Spirit and the gifts waiting inside you. Each practise is broken down into a meditation to connect to Spirit, energy work in Spirit and an action to implement. I love to journal my meditations so I can record significant feelings and messages. I recommend you start a journal to record your journey.

Connection to Spirit Meditation

Exercise #14

Take a deep breath in through your nose and out your mouth.

Nice deep breaths concentrating on the flow in and out.

Breathing in and out...now breathing normally and concentrating on your breath in and out.

Visualise your flow of breath coming up the spine and down the heart to the belly button. Breathe in through your nose, down through your heart and deeper into your stomach and out back up the spine and out your mouth. See this cycle as you breathe.

As you breathe, notice how your heart expands with every breath. See how your heart becomes brighter. Imagine your heart as a flower or lotus that is unfolding with every intentional breath you give.

Expand and open your heart fully and let your heart sing to you.

Listen to your heart's song.

Stay for a while in your heart's music.

Feel the musical notes of your heart's song fill your body. Feel it surge through every cell. Feel it pour out around your body like a cocoon.

You are love and love is you. Notice how you love everything about your body, cells, skin, hair, fingers, arms, chest, tummy, thighs, legs and feet.

You are the gift of Spirit. You are love. Trust in your instincts. Let love be your justifier and your bravery. Let love be the foundation to every relationship you have.

We give gratitude to the gifts of Spirit and the place it has in our heart.

Take a deep breath in through your nose and out your mouth.

Nice deep breaths, concentrating on the flow in and out.

Come back into your body feeling every sensation and remembering your message.

Now open your eyes.

_____

_____

_____

This energy work evokes the essence of Spirit. So when we turn on this energy, clarity and direction are revealed. If you find yourself feeling a little stuck or out of flow with a decision, project or stressed out from other things going on in your life, this exercise will help you see the truth in every issue and bring you clarity and direction.

To evoke the essence of Spirit, I practise the heart globe exercise. The heart globe exercise requires us to turn on a light in our hearts and keep this light contained to harness the essence of Spirit. By contained, I refer to the light having an edge or container. Containment is necessary in keeping everything within rather than spewing out everywhere. When we are not contained it reminds me of a leak in a tyre and it deflates. No matter how much air you pump back into it, it's hard work to keep it inflated, and you quickly lose energy or focus. Without containment, we lose the ability to get clarity.

This exercise has worked brilliantly in writing this book. When I feel writers block coming, I go into my heart and switch on my light.

Heart Globe

Exercise #15

Intentionally breathe into your heart space or heart chakra. Breathe in and out and feel your heart expand. Keep you intention in your heart and when you can feel your heart space, imagine there is a light globe in your heart and turn it on. Let this light expand throughout your heart, beaming

PART 4 - Te Mana

out your chest and back. Keep this light contained by imagining a light ring running arms width out from your heart and back. This will contain the energy to concentrate on your issues.

When you feel your light bright and contained, place any thoughts, decision or issues you may have into your heart globe. Intentionally keep your ideas, thoughts or decisions in this area. Breathe in and out and allow it to expand in your heart. This heart light shows up all the issues that you placed in this area. Open your heart fully and embrace all that is revealed. Sit with the feeling of having all revealed in the light. Allow Spirit to help you get clarity and direction. Clarity will come when you have fully surrendered and opened your heart to allow Spirit to flow through you. You will know the answer when it feels like it came from within and not from your headspace.

(If you find you keep going up into your head, place your hand on top of your head as if to put a lid on it).

Your practise right now is to turn on your heart globe, keep it contained and start using it for any decisions or choices that you need to make this week. The more you practise the heart globe, the easier it will become.

_____

_____

_____

Try this...

Exercise #16

When you are listening to conversations or when some one is talking to you, let their words land in your heart. Make sure your heart globe is on and contained and see how people react to you.

_____

_____

_____

PART 5

Te Mauri

Chapter 7:
Impulse – Te Mauri – The Union

"There is a universal, intelligent, life force that exists within everyone and everything. It resides within each one of use as a deep wisdom, an inner knowing. We can access this wonderful source of knowledge and wisdom through our intuition, an inner sense that tells us what feels right and true for us at any given moment."
Shakti Gawain

Impulse or the Mauri, is my favourite essence. In the online Maori dictionary it is *"the life principle, vital essence, source of emotions and an essential quality and vitality of a being or entity."* Beautifully described I would say. Growing up, I heard of Mauri as the life force that was within us and that is exactly what it is, but I did not fully understand the depth of what life force was or where it lived within me. It just seemed to be this mystical essence we were all born with that is likened to the soul, the thing that gives us life and vitality. It is and it isn't. It is an essence, but it is not the soul essence.

As explained in chapter 4, all three core elements make up the soul. As a young girl sitting in the Marae (Maori meeting house) and listening to the elder men speak, they would always start with *"Tihei Mauri Ora."* This phrase means "the sneeze of life," which describes the first breath, cough, or cry when a child is born and given their first introduction to the world. When the elders use it before they speak, they are claiming the right to stand and be heard. I guess when a child is born, their first breath or sound is a claim to be living.

PART 5 - Te Mauri

The Gift

I term the Impulse the union as it has neither a female nor male essence. It is both and it is neither. The union is where both the feminine and masculine energies are created and return home. It is the womb, the universal womb and it resides about 2-3 inches below the navel and about 1-2 inches inward for both men and women. In traditional Chinese medicine, the Impulse is in the lower dantian; I am going to refer to this space as Impulse. Impulse is the gift of life force and it is the base and foundation of the three core elements. This is where the other two elements will come to recharge, expand and create.

Impulse...(divine message)

The Impulse to create life is the greatest gift. The Impulse to create the life you love. The Impulse to love the life you live. This gift is the life force that is fire. It burns desire, passion and purpose. Your life force will set you free if you choose to listen to your inner desires and passions. You will feed the fire of purpose through creativity and love.

In the creation story, the mother (Nothingness) and father's (Darkness) union became the universal womb. Their close and tight embrace was the home and womb for their many children. When Great Spirit (Io) gifted the primal laws (Time and Change), he gave them freedom to move and expand. When he gifted the primal laws the three essences, he gave them a homing device, which is the Impulse (Mauri) to find their parents, embrace in the universal womb. The creation story highlights the universal womb as the feminine and masculine union. In their feminine and masculine union, there were surges of energy, movement and creativity as the universe was coming to light.

The Impulse of man is his direct line to Great Spirit, the God source or the "I AM." The God source is the union of the Nothingness and the Darkness where Great Spirit poured his love and intention to create. It is a direct link to the true source of Great Spirit, God or the creator's true intentions: LOVE.

The Virtues

Impulse works with the virtues of passion, purpose and creativity. Impulse holds and fires up your passions and ignites creativity. It has the innate imprint of your purpose that is etched on your first breath from birth. The great question when we come to a turning point in our lives is, "What is my purpose in life?" The answer is in the essence of Impulse. Most people would say the answer lies in your heart, but it actually lies in the space of Impulse in the sacral chakra. This energy centre is responsible for sensuality and sexuality, passion and creativity.

It is joy, so why would we not want to be living from these values?

Because for so long we have been taught not too. We have been taught to shame our sexuality and tame our creativity, be the same and not to stand out. But this is no longer in the surge of new energy that Earth has evolved into, and if you are an awakened soulful leader, then you will feel the need to live by the example that Impulse intends. The saying, live the life you love, is a perfect motto for the essence of Impulse. In living the life you love, Impulse will highlight your purpose. When you understand your purpose, you take on a whole new sense of passion and embrace this passion through creativity. Creativity is the pursuit to act upon your passion to be in your purpose. Love before purpose to authentically be on your path.

Love...(divine message)

Love is the centre of all creation. It is the light when you are lost in the darkness. It is the seed of all creations being birthed into the world. If you cannot feel and experience the love, how can you fully create and sustain life and energy. Connect to all things you love, surround yourself in this energy, and wonders will open before you.

Universal Intention

The Impulse is the return to home mechanism. Great Spirit created this essence to allow the children of the Nothingness and the Darkness to return to their parents, loving embrace in the universal womb. Great Spirit also created this mechanism in all of us, so when we need help or a loving embrace, we can connect to this source of the universal womb and all its wisdom. Impulse becomes a return home mechanism when you are living through love. Loving first will set you on a path to your passion. Passion is the intensity of being in the energy of love. In the passion, you will find your purpose. Live passionately and you will find purpose in all you do.

Purpose will be your mantra. It will be a way of doing and a way of living. Purpose gives us reasons for doing things in this lifetime. My purpose gave me a stronger connection to Great Spirit. It gave me strength to believe in myself as Great Spirit believes in me. When I needed support to keep moving in my path, I was able to connect to the God source and recharge my energy because being in purpose is not easy. It's scary, frustrating and risky.

It is also responsibility. What I feel most when I am on purpose is so responsible. Great Spirit has entrusted me with the responsibility to awaken and teach soulful leaders. I was brought here to teach the teachers because I am passionate about the wellbeing and education of our children. At times, I wish I didn't have this responsibility and sometimes I wish I could go back to regular work and make a small difference, but I know I cannot. I would not be living the universal intention of Impulse and I know I will not be living the life I love.

Real-World Intention

The real world of living in Impulse is damn scary. Being in purpose is a huge responsibility and living up to that responsibility is friggen hard. I look at mentors and other people who are on purpose, and I wonder how I will ever get to that point in my life. I am in spiritual purpose. I know exactly what I am here to do, but my emotional self is just frightened. I am frightened to be standing in the light of my own wisdom. I am afraid of being seen, and probably most afraid of being told I am a load of BS. I know that what I know is authentic and real. I live by the law of practice what you preach and be the shining example that others want to be, so why the doubt?

Connecting to Impulse has taught me that these fears are valid and okay, as all my mentors and people I admire have had the same doubts in their lifetime. Impulse intends for you to move or act. Move into your power, your passion and your purpose. Impulse allows you to recognise every aspect of your fear and place it in the energy of the movement and in the Impulse. Honestly, this realisation was scary at first because I did not want to take my fear into my body thinking it would engulf me in a cloud of darkness. Quite the opposite, really: by becoming aware of my emotional fear and giving it to Impulse and containing it there, I was able to see the energetic and physical steps I needed to take to make that fear a little less scary.

Impulse's intention to move in baby steps whilst in fear has helped me move forward towards my dreams and passion. Along with the intention to move or action, is the intention to be creative. Creativity feeds the desire to want more of your passion or dreams. So with contained fear it allows me to move forward and action goals and in turn, I create more of what I want, which feeds more passion. I love Impulse to get stuff done.

In and out of flow

Being IN the flow of Impulse is a direct alignment with your passion and purpose. You will feel like you are moving quite quickly towards your goals and taking great action steps to get where you need to be. Maybe you got the position or promotion you were aiming for, or you are really positioning yourself as the expert in your field. Being in flow still means you feel your fear, but it is easy to cope with and less taxing on your emotions. The IN flow energy is a wonderful feeling that can recharge your energy centres when you are in gratitude. A gratitude attitude keeps the IN flow for longer.

When you are OUT of flow with Impulse you will feel discouraged to move into your purpose or passion. This is when we allow our fear to take over and stop ourselves from moving forward. Sometimes we may take a different route and say, "Well, that didn't work so I'll try this." This was my routine for a while, trying different things because my fear was still taking over and I only realised this when I found myself on a treadmill of creativity with no output. I kept creating the next new thing, so it felt like I was moving and actioning, but what I was actually doing was running in circles and not confronting the uncomfortable or the fog. In this space of OUT of flow, you feel drained because you feel you have tried everything, but you're just tired of running on the creativity treadmill. This treadmill can make you feel airy-fairy and ungrounded, not knowing which direction to go.

It is great to be aware of the IN and OUT flow of this energy because you can then pull yourself out and reassess where you are right now and do something energetically to get back IN to flow. I wish I knew this information sooner. I wouldn't have taken so long to get onto the right path of my business. Instead I ran on the creativity treadmill for 2 years before realising what I was doing. I'm sure my loved ones and friends were thinking there she goes again with another one of her ideas.

Being OUT of flow heeds great lessons for leaders. Only soulful leaders willing to reflect on themselves will see the OUT flow as a chance to improve. Whether the energy moves IN or OUT, it will always flow, surge or move and we gain universal wisdom from each tide. Opening Spirit or Mana with Impulse or Mauri to the fog and confusion of an OUT of flow will allow us to see its truth (whether we like it or not) act with justice and integrity.

Flow...(divine message)

Do not deny yourself the flow of Impulse. The true flow is between you and the universal wisdom that is available to all. Do not be discouraged by the veil of fog, for in this veil lies true courage and determination to continue your purpose. Release all confusion and fear to Impulse. Let it go to the source of wisdom and return to you cleansed and infused with purposeful creativity.

Energy Work with Impulse

These practises will help connect to the essence of Impulse and open the channel to the abundance of universal wisdom. It's a great idea to journal straight after a meditation so you can record your thoughts, feelings and messages.

Connection to Impulse meditation

Exercise #17

Take a deep breath in through your nose and out your mouth.

Nice deep breaths concentrating on the flow in and out.

PART 5 - Te Mauri

Breathing in and out...now breathing normally and concentrating on your breath in and out.

Visualise your breath going to the Impulse, 2-3 inches below your navel and 3 inches inward and see the flow of breath coming out, like a cycle. Breathe in through your nose, down through your heart and into Impulse and out back up the spine and out your mouth. See this cycle as you breathe.

As you breathe into the Impulse, notice a golden pearl. Feel how the pearl surges with movement and joy. Notice the sensuality of every energetic movement. Feel the passion created from every movement the pearl makes.

See the pearl glowing and allow the energy to expand and fill the entire area of Impulse and come out all around you about an arms length away.

Stay for a while in this expansive and creative energy.

Feel the creativity of Impulse fill your body. Feel it surge through every cell. Feel it pour out around your body like a cocoon.

You are love and passion. Your passion will lead you to a purposeful life. You will create in the universal wisdom that is intended for you.

Listen to this inner wisdom. Let it whisper to every cell in your body to awaken the purpose that was etched on your first breathe of life. Feel every cell in your body enliven with an awakened wisdom.

We give gratitude to the gifts of Impulse and the place it has in our body.

Take a deep breath in through your nose and out your mouth.

Nice deep breaths concentrating on the flow in and out.

Come back into your body feeling every sensation and remembering your message.

Now open your eyes.

_____

_____

_____

Working with the energy of Impulse gets you back IN the flow and it's all about confronting the unknown or the fog. The fog is the confusion. If you have created something that you thought was the right thing to do but it had an undesirable outcome, then confront the confusion around it. In leadership, it may be not enough capacity building or consultation. In business, it may be not enough marketing or the wrong marketing message. Whatever it may be, bring the fog into the space of Impulse within your body and contain it there.

Remember containment is to put the fog or confusion into a container of some sort and hold this image in the Impulse. It could be a bubble or cloud: whatever you resonate with. Once you have the fog contained within Impulse, allow the energy to surround it, shape it and infuse it. The universal intention will connect you to the true source of your wisdom and the real-world intention will get the energy moving again. Allow the answers to flow without expectations. Flow will begin once you release it to the essence of Impulse. Below is the full energetic exercise to work with the energy of Impulse, and I call it the pearl of wisdom.

Pearl of wisdom

Exercise #18

Intentionally breathe into the Impulse or sacral chakra. Breathe in and out and feel the space of the Impulse. (Most people have never felt the Impulse before, so it may take some time to feel this space). Keep your intention on

PART 5 - Te Mauri

Impulse and when you feel this space, imagine a golden pearl right in the centre. Feel this golden pearl illuminating golden light throughout Impulse and an arms width around you. Remember to contain the energy surrounding you by placing a ring or bubble around the illuminated golden light.

When you feel Impulse bright and contained, release any fears, issues or intentions into this space. Intentionally keep whatever you have placed in the Impulse contained in this area. Breathe in and out and allow the pearl to surge through whatever you are releasing. Feel the energetic excitement and flow of the wisdom being awakened. It's important to continue to keep this energetic flow contained. If it is not contained, we can lose focus and get sidetracked by another creative thing. Allow the wisdom to reveal itself in the golden glow of Impulse. The answer will always be revealed from within your body and not from your headspace. It will feel like deep and grounded wisdom.

Your practise right now is to feel that pearl of wisdom and illuminate it in Impulse.

_____

_____

_____

Try this...

Exercise #19

Practise keeping it illuminated and contained and check in through out the day.

Notice surges of excitement or changes in energy coming from the pearl. Write in a journal what you discover.

_____

_____

_____

PART 6

Te Maui

Chapter 8:
Insight – The Masculine

"Don't try to comprehend with your mind. Your minds are very limited. Use your intuition."
Madeleine L'Engle

Interestingly enough, I researched the meaning of Maui and all I could find are the descriptions of the Maori Legend demi-god, Maui Tikitiki a Taranga, and his deeds. Considering it is one of Great Spirit's greatest gifts, the demi-god has over-shadowed the essence of Insight. Te Maui is Insight and the essence is supreme understanding of oneness. Insight is the understanding of elegance and flow, rhythm and tide and most importantly, how we are connected to all of it. Great Spirit gifted Insight to bind all that was created together with balance and harmony. It is the concept of survival and a balanced eco-system. Life and death are in the careful balance and renewal of Insight.

The Gift

The gift of Insight is a masculine essence because it resides in the area of logic and thought. The pineal gland or the third eye chakra is the energy centre of Insight, the third gift of Great Spirit. Beyond the physical human residence of Insight, it is masculine because of the essence of its true gift: survival. This isn't a primitive survival mechanism, but more of a recognition of the world and universe we are a part of. I say "a part" as in you make up the core of every other living being and flowing river on this planet, including the stars that blaze miles away in our solar system. This is a hard concept for many to grasp and it is a little like *The Matrix* movie, where everything is not real, time doesn't exist and you are the chosen one.

PART 6 - Te Maui

My culture and other indigenous cultures lived by the lore of the universe and respected all living creatures, including those they killed to give food for their hungry families. A prayer of abundance and good fortune was done before the hunt, fish or gather and a prayer of thanks after gathering food or after the kill. The prayer was a sign of respect and gratitude for offering (I say this in a universal sense) themselves to feed their family. Society has desensitised the way we feel for the food we eat. Just like the saying out of sight and out of mind, we become disconnected with the true essence of Insight.

Connected...(divine message)

We are all connected to this vast universe, every planet, rock, plant, and living being. We are connected through the same source or God light of creation. When each life is born on Earth, we celebrate in their journey and when we die, the heavens celebrate our journey and the light is replenished. Know your life is part of a grander architecture that you have a major role in playing. Do not let the little things get in the way of being grand because you are the chosen one.

In the creation story, Great Spirit gifted Insight (Maui) to bring harmony and balance to the surging electricity of Impulse (Mauri). When Insight saw the beauty in the creation of the stars and planets, Insight began connecting everything he saw with a silver thread of Great Spirit's light so each living creation knew they were a part of another.

We have the ability to travel along these silver threads to communicate, see and feel people and places. Tohunga (Shaman) were able to use these silver threads to see the first explorers before they even got to the shores of Aotearoa (New Zealand). This knowledge and skill was exclusive only to Matakite (seer or clairvoyant) and Tohunga (Shaman), as they were the only people to have such a sacred connection to the spirit world. The new world has awakened many soulful leaders to its wonder and we are more curious than ever to see how far this wonder will expand.

The Virtues

Insight works with the virtues of balance and harmony. It's so simple, yet one of the hardest things to live by. There are great lessons in living in harmony for the world, yet we find this hard to do with ourselves. Our worst enemy can be our own self-doubt. As leaders, we often self-sabotage what we do because we have not learnt to live in harmony with our own judgement. Judgement is merely a mechanism that can help us reflect on our actions. But sadly, that's just not the way we use judgement. Judgement from others has a negative affect on how we judge ourselves and how we judge others. The truth is judgement is not meant for you to give anyone else but yourself. Remember, Great Spirit gave us our own judge when he gifted Spirit (Mana). We are to judge our own actions through unconditional love for whom we truly are and what we were bought here to do. Judgement is supposed to be gentle, loving and for our reflection only.

I know people love to call it reflection, and this is because of the negative connotation that judgement has on it and it can be your number one block that holds you back from becoming the leader you are meant to be or fulfilling the dream you know you were meant to live. Our fear of judgement by others can cripple your dreams and aspirations. Know that judgement is meant for you only. It doesn't matter what others think because they will see you how they want to see you anyway. Soulful leaders will judge what they do with love and will gain clarity on where they could improve or do better. This is how they begin to live in harmony with themselves.

Balancing your life and career can be a juggling act and that's what it's meant to be. There is no hiding the fact that life is about ups and downs, twists and turns, but it's really about how quickly you can pick yourself back up again and keep moving. Balancing your world and every aspect of it from environment, capabilities, behaviours, beliefs and values and identity is key to fulfilling a happy and harmonious life.

PART 6 - Te Maui

It is important to note that being in balance does not mean that you are happy and positive all the time in any aspect. There are flashes of anger, sadness and fear. Every emotion is a valid emotion and it's okay, but too much of one emotion can create a sense of neediness or falseness and none of these serve your purpose as a soulful leader. If you find yourself getting caught up in drama or gossip sessions at work, this creates a sense of distrust and falseness. If you find you are not putting yourself forward or you need constant reassurance of your talents or the choices you make, then this can create a sense of neediness.

At the core of falseness is ego and at the core of neediness is fear and as explained in the previous chapter, these are the two emotions that we find out of control in leadership. Insight can help us value the connection we have with the people in our lives. The more we feel connected, ego and fear becomes less. Embracing the connection to all living things is true balance and harmony.

Universal Intention

Insight is connection to all things. Great Spirit created this essence to allow the children of the Darkness and the Nothingness to know they are all connected and bound to all the beauty before them. Understanding this connection enabled all the children to live in balance and harmony with one another and their surroundings. Survival itself is pure balance and harmony with our environment. Insight is within all of us, primarily in the gift of survival. This gift is so strong in our evolution that it has its own part in our brains called the "amygdala" or "fight or flight" mechanism.

The amygdala is involved in the automatic responses associated with emotion and emotional behaviour. The amygdala is also responsible for fear conditioning and storing those memories associated with an emotional experience. It can feel fear and perceive it in others. Today the amygdala is being controlled by anger, hate and sadness. Our new world survival is surviving ourselves and the destruction we create. Because this part of the brain has been adapted or altered, it has a huge effect on our connectedness to each other and our environment. We need to re-connect with this part of our brain to stimulate its natural and innate response to emotion, thus opening up channels or silver threads of connectivity. It is easy to bring back this connection, but it takes practice. I will show you how in the practise section.

Real-World Intention

It is Great Spirit's intention for us to live on this beautiful planet in balance and harmony. Even in our human evolution our greatest lesson is to continue living in balance and harmony while surviving our own creations. Ultimately, we create everything around us from an emotional, physical and a spiritual perspective. We create the way we feel through how we sense it in our pineal gland, then respond to it in our amygdala and we play out a physical reaction, whether it is happiness, violence or illness.

What has happened over time is the pineal gland, is becoming desensitised due to our current lifestyle. We have cut off a lot of sensory experiences for many reasons, including childhood experiences, environmental conditioning, and our fast-paced lifestyle, just to name a few. When we shut down the senses, we disconnect from the amygdala, which creates a less conscious form of experiencing events in our lives. For example, it can cause a limiting belief system that does not serve a greater good. It can also cause a number of emotional behaviours like depression and anger.

Research shows that people who suffer from bipolar disorder have slightly enlarged amygdala. This shows when there is a brain imbalance, it causes emotional imbalance in the body. If we are not feeling the sensations in the body, we stay in the headspace of our minds and the other energy centres shut down because no energy flow is reaching these areas. The headspace uses all the energy just thinking about things that might, could have or did happen. The energy is used in thoughts that mostly are irrelevant because of their timing, instead of being used to experience an emotion or being present in the moment of the event. We don't spend long enough experiencing something fully where it comes back to your body in pleasure. The pleasure of music when the birds sing to each other, the pleasure of smells that make your mouth water and send every cell in your body into a desirable frenzy. You could say we take most of these simple pleasures for granted today and the problem with taking things for granted is we lose the connection to Insight.

The real-world intention is to feel the connection we have to our surroundings and understand our gift within it. We need to stimulate and re-energise the connection between the pineal gland and the amygdala to activate sensory pleasure in the body and open up the third eye intention of balance and harmony. To do this, we need to change the way we experience our thoughts and channel our energy into our senses. When a situation or event happens, we make ourselves aware of an emotional reaction. The emotional reaction is then felt in the body and these sensations are bought back to the awareness of the brain. It is an energetic cyclic flow that travels through the body and back to the brain. I call it cognitive mindfulness that creates a learning sensation. In this case we are learning to feel sensations in our body to stimulate connection between the pineal gland and amygdala. Doing this practise will re-energise the pineal gland and the amygdala.

In and out of flow

The IN and OUT flow spectrum of Insight can go from extreme delight and happiness to manic depressive and suicidal tendencies. Being at the far end of the OUT of flow spectrum of the gift of Insight questions our very existence. We become disconnected to who we really are, our dreams and aspirations and then we disconnect from the world around us. This is a common cycle for people who suffer from depression. Anger and depression is a sign that the essence of Insight is out of balance or blocked. Humans innately need to belong or be part of something, so when we distance or close off this part of the human psyche, we are severing the silver threads that connect all things together. Suicidal thoughts can occur when the silver threads are severed and this is not a good place to be.

At the lighter end of the OUT of flow spectrum of Insight is a common area that I have found myself in many times over in my life, which is a lack of balance between my own wants and needs and the wants and needs of my job, business, family and friends. I feel this happens because I am a mother and want to nurture and keep my family and friends safe and happy. In doing this, I generally put myself last and don't follow through with the things I truly desire or want. So what actually happens is I feel resentment because I am running around for everyone, then I feel drained, lacking in energy until I eventually snap. By snap I mean lose it, start yelling and screaming at everyone because I have to work and take care of everything else, no one will clean their mess or do as I've asked (usually poor kids cop this one). Then I move on to my husband and tell him he doesn't appreciate all I do and I feel like I'm the only parent (blah, blah, blah) you get it.

The thing is, I caused myself to lose it by not honouring my desires and needs. I blamed everyone around me, usually my family. This is a fine balancing act of the flow of Insight. If we do not listen, share or feed our own desires and dreams, but do so much to feed the desires of those in our lives, then we become resentful. Resentment is not a good energy to be holding within your body as it takes you further down the OUT of flow spectrum of Insight. Listening to what you want and acting on it one little step at a time will balance out this essence.

Being IN the flow of this essence is absolutely blissful and I mean blissful. When you understand how Insight works for you, you will not look back, maybe a couple times, but you will know how to bring yourself back to a

PART 6 - Te Maui

more blissful place. IN flow satisfies the innate need to belong, to contribute and be part of something. The silver threads of your intuition begin to surge with energy. You know exactly who you are and what you want and most importantly, the little steps to get there. You understand the grand plan and your place within it. When you ride this silver thread that was weaved specifically for you within your universe, you will not want to get off. Your silver thread of connectedness will bring you peace, clarity and happiness because you have a sense of pleasure from following your desires.

You belong...(divine message)

You have a unique place in this universe. You belong to a collective of universal souls and you are never alone. You are as grand as the mightiest mountain and unique as the tiniest creature. There is much for you to see. Take time to observe the beauty that surrounds you and know that you are part of this grand architecture of life. The silver connectors link all divine souls together with divine beauty. Each one sings a harmonious melody that hypnotically calls to you to follow its silver lining. Open your inner thoughts to the possibility of something greater. Do not limit yourself to small mindedness and self-doubt. You are here for great things and you have all the divine help you need.

Energy Work with Insight

These practises will enliven the senses and bring sensations of pleasure into your body. When I talk about pleasure, it is the harmony of all your senses being brought into the moment for you to experience. Don't forget to journal your experiences.

Connection to Insight meditation

Exercise #20

To do this meditation, you will need to visualise the following before you start. You may want to practise the visualisations before you start (see figure 1 and 2).

Figure 1. Flat V (lying flat)

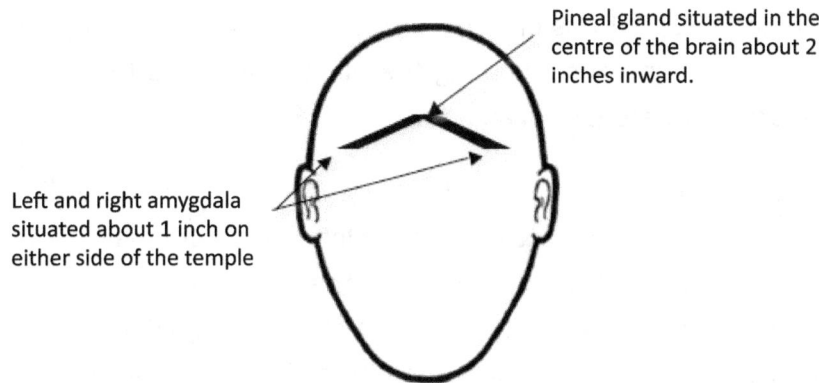

Pineal gland situated in the centre of the brain about 2 inches inward.

Left and right amygdala situated about 1 inch on either side of the temple

Figure 2. Figure 8's

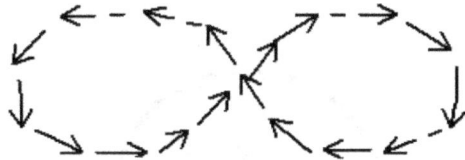

Take a deep breath in through your nose and out your mouth.

Nice deep breathes concentrating on the flow in and out.

Breathing in and out...now breathing normally and concentrating on your breath in and out.

PART 6 - Te Maui

Visualise a flat V where the middle point is touching the pineal gland (located in the centre of your head about 2 inches inward) and the other ends touching the right and left amygdala (located by the temples about 1 inch inward and directly behind the eye socket). Continue breathing steadily in and out.

When you visualise the V, breathe in down the right line of the amygdala, and breathe out to the pineal gland (middle point), breathe in down the left line of the amygdala and then breathe out back to the pineal gland (middle point). Repeat this breathing pattern until you feel a rhythm and connection between your breathing the pineal gland and the amygdala. Continue breathing steadily in and out.

Now visualise a figure 8 on the right V line from the pineal gland to the right amygdala and another figure 8 on the left V line from the pineal gland to the left amygdala. Now breathe simultaneously along the figure 8s in the same directional flow. You may want to place a golden ball or light along the figure 8s to get the right breathing direction. If it's out of sync when you start, that's okay, just continue to breathe, slowing down your breath and you will find your rhythm. (See figure 3).

Figure 3. Figure 8 breathing from pineal gland to the amygdala.

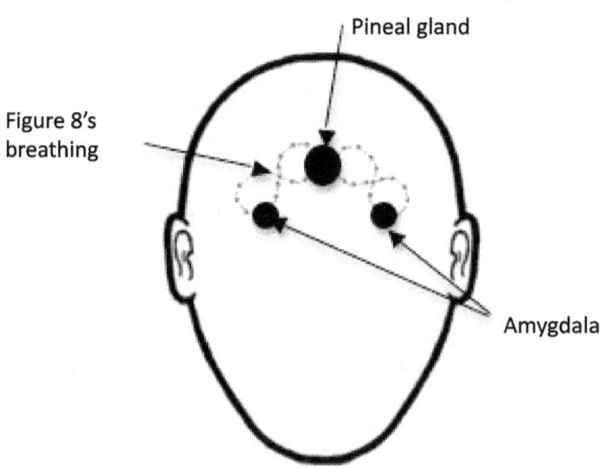

Feel the pineal gland and the amygdala surging with energy as you breathe. Feel the pleasure awakening and enlivening your senses. When you breathe in, feel every sensation in your body awaken. When you breathe out, feel every cell alive with life. Become aware of your senses within your surroundings, notice which senses are heightened right now. Become aware of your connectedness to things around you. Allow Insight to flow through your body. Feel the connection in your third eye expand in awareness of your senses.

We give gratitude to the gifts of Insight and the awareness it enlivens us with in our body.

Take a deep breath in through your nose and out your mouth.

Nice deep breaths concentrating on the flow in and out.

Come back into your body feeling every sensation and remembering your message.

Now open your eyes.

_____

_____

_____

Working with the energy of Insight is IN flow magnetised and there is still so much more to do with it, but that's for another book. This energy is harmony and it is achieved when we work with the connection of the parts of the brain that have been disconnected, which in turn dulls our sensory experiences and can limit our beliefs.

Using this energy in leadership is mastering balance and harmony in life and in work. This is not easy, especially when we try to separate the different roles we have in our life. Believe it or not, there's only one role to play, and that is the lead role of your life and the difference that you want to make in it. Other hats or masks are only illusions and are a cover up of what we do not want others to see. Insight energy will give you a strong sense of who you are and your place in the world. Being anything other than this will only dull and limit your sensory experiences. In other words, it will feel crappy.

Golden Projector

Exercise #21

The more you practise the meditation or just conscious breathing using the V and figure 8 breathing, the more you will strengthen connection to the gifts of Insight. Once you have made the amygdala and pineal gland connection and you feel it, try this practise I call the Golden Projector. This practise will prepare you for other practises in this book.

Intentionally breathe into Insight, seeing the rhythm and flow of the energy between the pineal gland and the amygdala. Visualise the V glowing with golden light then feel this light stretching out in front of you about arm's length through your eyes and the third eye coming from the pineal gland. Visualise this light in the shape of a triangle from your third eye, down to your eyes and across the bridge of your nose (see figure 3), like a projector lamp shining out in front of you. Notice where this light wants to go and how you feel when your golden projector is on. I feel my intuition heightened and I could move things with my mind (I haven't yet...yet).

Figure 4. Golden projector

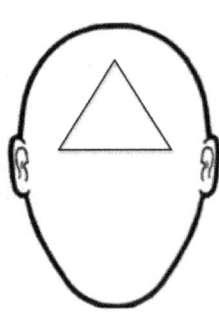

Try this...

Exercise #22

Your practise right now is to consciously breathe into Insight using the V and figure 8 directional breathing. Do this as much as you can throughout the day. Notice what happens for you or what starts to change. Note how people react to you or how you react to people around you. Write in your journal what you discover.

PART 7

The Blueprint

Chapter 9:
Understanding The 3 Core Elements

"Put your heart, mind, and soul into even your smallest acts. This is the secret of success."
Swami Sivananda

The three core elements or life force are amazing energy centres to work with on their own and when combined and used in sync with each other, they become a powerhouse of magic. Mana, Mauri and Maui (Spirit, Impulse and Insight) are core elements that dictate our human experiences, but they work in our highest benefit if we work with the energy they possess. The three core elements of native wisdom are the blueprint of all things created, from the plant kingdom to the animal kingdom. The creation story unlocks this information in Great Spirit's grand architecture and organisation of the universe. Innately we are given the blueprint for all creation, including the things we create within our lives from the way we live to how we live. The reason I wrote this book was to unlock the blueprint for the awakening of Soulful Leaders and those who choose to listen to the native wisdom within these words.

For centuries, my people have guarded these stories through rituals and chants. The stories were considered so sacred in knowledge that only Tohunga (shaman) or Matakite (seerer or healer) would be privy to the content and power it held. I was curious to why these narratives were only privy to Tohunga and Matakite, and I can only conclude two theories. The first theory is Tohunga and Matakite had a connection to the divine that came with a deeper understanding of its laws and teachings. The second theory is no one else wanted it.

PART 7 - The Blueprint

What they didn't want was the responsibility and sacrifice that came with the undertaking of such knowledge and teachings. Most Tohunga and Matakite sacrificed great heartache and pain to attain this status and wealth of pure knowledge. My father shared many stories of our people and the sacrifices made to their initiation into Tohungaship (the art of shamanism). My great-great-grandfather was supposed to be next inline to take the Tohunga teachings and knowledge from his father. Because of his status as having this gift, he was blamed for putting a makutu (curse) on a young child who died. He knew the stigma of this event would curse him for a long time and he chose to leave his hapu (clan). He chose not to have the gift (or curse) of Tohunga, so he followed the Catholic faith. Of course he did not curse the baby, but it does show the fear in a community of those that posses such knowledge.

In many of the stories I have heard growing up, Tohunga and Matakite come with much fear and misunderstanding of the true nature of their responsibility. There was fear among our own people and those who were born responsible guardians of the knowledge now had an outlet to join the missionaries in their quest for assimilation into a better world (a little sarcasm here). During assimilation into this better world was the outlawing of Tohunga or Matakite practices. This was the demise of my people's spiritual practices, and thus its purity was forever forgotten.

Until now...

Spiritual DNA

The truth of this evolutionary change is that the information is never truly lost if we are all inherently the owners of the universal blueprint. What we needed was time to develop whatever information we needed to be ready for this particular time and this information includes our DNA structure. Our DNA is made up of 2 strands that scientists know of called the double helix.

What spiritual teachings tells us, including biblical teachings, is that God breathed life into us, therefore structuring our human bodies with earthly DNA and spiritual DNA in light of himself, which has been termed the God DNA. Scientists originally only looked at the 2 DNA strands and termed the other 10 strands as "junk" because of their dormant nature. Spiritualists have long said that the awakening of spiritual DNA is the evolution of the new spiritual human being. A boy from Nuneaton, Warwickshire, in the UK was born with 3 DNA strands, which has been the first ever recorded. This has baffled doctors and scientists, but I can't help feeling that it is just part of the human evolution and the awakening of our innate blueprint.

Russian researchers have explored the remaining 90% of our DNA that has been termed "junk" because of its apparent dormancy and have discovered the genetic code for these DNA strands follows the rules for linguistics. Experimental research proved living DNA tissue will always respond to language modulated laser rays and even to radio waves. Plainly put, our DNA can be influenced and reprogrammed by words and frequencies. This explains why affirmations, hypnosis and the like affect humans and their bodies. As a teacher for over 10 years, I would have never thought that my knowledge of syntax, semantics and basic grammar rules had the power to alter and reprogram DNA. If only I knew the code to unlock this limitless potential in students, however, I used and continue to use the power of affirmations daily.

My point is, in all this discussion we hold the blueprint to creativity and ultimately limitless potential. So if we understand what creativity is, what is limitless potential? The answer to that question lies within each individual. Each individual has chosen their parents, partners and family in this present life to experience certain situations that can repair and restore their spiritual DNA. We have chosen our life path to put ourselves in situations that can inevitably set us up for evolutionary success. We

PART 7 - The Blueprint

can't evolve backwards (I hope) so we can only move forward. If the DNA is a storage unit of information and the blueprint of life and creation, then we hold limitless potential to create whatever it is we desire.

It's grand and wonderful knowing that we have a blueprint that contains limitless potential for us to create our deepest desires, but how do we tap into this limitless source or even understand how to make the blueprint work for our situations? This is the problem we have, knowing how to make this work in any given situation or when the shit really hits the fan of life.

How do we get ourselves out of the shit and onto the beach (if you like beaches)?

It's all about acting on the knowledge you receive. There is no point in learning something to not put it into practice. Whilst learning is great and I absolutely love learning, it can be an excuse not to put things into action. For a long time I would say I need to do this course or study for that course before I got to a point of that's enough. You have enough and you are enough. The excuse of learning stops us from getting out into the world and putting our knowledge into practice. It's great to learn, but your learning must be actioned in order for you to best help yourself or someone else. Without practice or action we do not become the leaders that this world needs. This world needs leaders that are willing to act on things that are important in the lives of those around us. So let's understand this blueprint better so we can help those around us.

Great Spirit infused each of us with the internal blueprint to limitless knowledge and potential, however, when we came onto the dense earthly plain, we forgot all knowledge and, most importantly, connection to Great Spirit himself. So all living things were gifted another layer of native wisdom and knowledge in order to live harmoniously on Earth.

Layers of Native Wisdom

Another native narrative and piece of native wisdom of my culture mentions "three baskets of knowledge and two sacred stones" that were given to humankind to help them understand and put into practice the innate life force that lies in each person. These baskets are common to use as a foundational framework when working in organisations in New Zealand. I have seen many councils and groups refer to these baskets as a framework or preamble to their work and the work they do for others. So these baskets are well known, but have varying interpretations according to different tribal connections. Overall, the essences of the baskets are the same.

There is a reason all our stories were held in high regard and kept pure and sacred for so long. It was because of the power and purity of the gifts told within them. When the Maori people inhabited New Zealand, our human evolution and the earth's evolution was still primitive and raw, hence the reason only certain people could deeply understand the gifts within the story. But in saying that, the people responsible for this knowledge were not always of a holistic humanitarian view. Because of the era of human evolution in leadership, my people were in between a hunter warrior and conquering lands for power position. So this sacred knowledge had the purpose of protection and war.

I guess you can only go for so long before a cleansing is due and in my people's case, it came in the form of the Crown. This cleansing I speak of was the taking away of Maori rights to practise their medicine, healing or Karakia (prayer). It wasn't totally lost, as a few special ones were still being

PART 7 - The Blueprint

given the teachings and knowledge. What I do know is that a time was coming in the earth's evolution where the awakened ones would return with the knowledge and teachings for all who wish to listen and learn. That time has arrived, as the Mayan calendar pre-determined.

December 2012 was another level of earth's ascension and not her demise as the media portrayed. As the earth ascends in an energetic journey every 13,000 years, she takes on a new form of energetic vibration and humankind living here can feel it. We are either feeling great with it or not. Unfortunately, the earth will weed out those who are not on the same vibrational level by making them feel uncomfortable, irritable, angry, hatred, depressed and in fear. Those feeling this way will make the choice on whether they stay and raise their energetic vibration or leave this earthly plain. Harsh, but that's the nuts and bolts of it.

Now is a great time to look back into native wisdom and cultural narratives and share the true essence of each teaching. Now that we understand the three core elements, essences or life force, it is the three baskets of knowledge that add another layer of native wisdom to understanding and using the three core elements. Tane, who ascended to the 12 heavens where Io (Great Spirit) resided, received the three baskets of knowledge and two stones.

Te Kete Tuauri, "beyond the world of darkness," is the basket of understanding what is behind our sensory experiences.

Te Kete Tuatea, "world beyond space and time," is the basket of knowledge of spirit and our connection to each other.

Te Kete Aronui, "that before us," is the basket of sensory awareness and experience or as I like to call it, learning sensations.

This interpretation is an awakened realisation of the layer in which these baskets help mankind re-connect to our leadership capacity and believe it or not, a connection with the divine is a necessary component of leadership success. These baskets of knowledge help us become acutely aware of our surroundings and our connections with others. This is where mindfulness comes into play. I see the three core elements or essences as deep soulful understanding and the three baskets as the mindfulness practices in order to live by Great Spirit's virtues and create balance, harmony and happiness in our lives. Each of the three baskets has a place in our body just like the three core elements. I like to think of these baskets as the mindfulness practice and knowledge that goes with each element.

Insight the masculine element, has the knowledge of Te Kete Tuauri, the basket beyond the world of darkness. This is the understanding of all things working in unison without our awareness or beyond our sense. Everything has a ritual on Earth, like seasons and lunar eclipses, but they happen beyond our thought process of them. This basket contains the prayers that align with these rituals to honour and give thanks to all the arrangements necessary to live in harmony on Earth. There are so many things to be mentioned in this basket, but it would take another book to write them. In short, Insight is our survival and connection to the greater architecture of life and the basket beyond the world of darkness are the rituals that happen beyond our awareness and practices of giving thanks and praise for our part in Earth's evolution. This is the practice of gratitude.

Spirit the feminine element, has the knowledge of Te Kete Tuatea, the basket of world beyond space and time. This is the understanding of our connection to spirit through love and peace. The heart is the keeper of truth and justice for human kind. Here we find how to love one another and live in peace. The basket of world beyond space and time teaches us to practice being in the present moment of love where we find peace. This is the practice of being present with love and honesty.

Impulse the union element, has the knowledge of Te Kete Aronui, the basket of that before us. This is the understanding of our learning sensations

PART 7 - The Blueprint

derived from cognitive mindfulness. Our bodies experience through our senses of what things taste like, how they feel, how they smell, what they sounds like and what they look like. These senses create an emotional experience, whether it's good or bad, and we transmit the experiences to our brains that store the information depending on how emotional the experience was. The basket of that before us teaches us to experience life through our senses to enliven every cell in the body. When we enliven our cells, we enliven the other energy centres too. Pleasure, joy and happiness are things humans are meant to experience. So is pain, even though we do not like the experience it creates, but nevertheless, we have the capacity to learn and teach from every learning sensation. This is the practice of cognitive mindfulness and learning sensations.

There are two sacred stones that accompany the baskets and represent the attainment of learning. They act as a placeholder or an acknowledgement to the beginning and end of the journey, not that the journey ever finishes, but it stands as a marker to pick up where you left off. These sacred stones from the heavens come with rituals to signify the importance and sacredness of the beginning of your journey and to celebrate the wisdom received. On a universal level, these two sacred stones represent the primal laws of time and change.

When we begin a journey or attain learning, we measure this in time (first stone placed at the beginning of the journey). The second stone represents the change or transformation attained from the knowledge received. The sacred stones in your life are always moving forward as you develop and grow through life lessons. Always notice the stone where you began your journey and be in gratitude of your growth through the primal laws of time and change. I see these stones as markers in our soulful transitions through life's journey and knowledge or lessons learned. As explained in chapter two these stones identify or signify soulful transitions.

Three Core Elements and Leadership

You may wonder why the three core elements are important in leadership. I have noticed in leadership theory and being involved in leadership roles that the three core elements are essential as a leader. When the three core elements are connected and activated, people will respond differently to you as a leader. The three core elements give leaders absolute conviction about who they are and what they stand for. Leaders stand out from others and their messages are heard. People align with soulful leaders, passion and want to follow them because this type of leader exudes wisdom, talent, sagacity and fairness.

Each element has so much wisdom entwined within that to not harness and use what is innately yours is not living the life you were born to. The three elements are your right to lead the life you love and we do this by allowing our gifts to shine through the guidance and practices of our blueprint or our soul. As I have mentioned, the three core elements working together is the soul and when we use the gifts and guidance of the soul, we become soulful leaders.

I know in previous educational leadership roles that I have been involved in, I did not honour my Spirit by seeking clarity and truth in pursuing projects and I know that at times I shut down the creativity of Impulse because I was being stubborn or negative about certain things, which closed off my connection or Insight to who I was really serving, which was my ego. Does this sound familiar? If you took a look around, it would be the majority of leaders in this world. You only have to open a newspaper or switch the TV on to the news and you will see this example everywhere.

I was leading a community group when I began the road to soulful leadership after leaving the education industry, and it was difficult establishing common values and core beliefs. But achievable. We began community consultation and building a following on the needs of what the community wanted and we established a media profile and rode the coat tails of a world wide indigenous cause, which increased our exposure. Things were going well, but it was a lot of work for a small community group trying to make

PART 7 - The Blueprint

impactful change. Previous members returned to the group as they saw interest and popularity was coming back to the community. Unfortunately their ego also sought to establish power within the group. So much so that it changed the energy and clarity of group members. Feeling this energy like a black cloud engulf all the light out of me, I had to make a decision. Knowing the hard work that had already gone into re-establishing the community and building it up to something wonderful was hard to let go of, but I could not work with this person, so I made the soulful decision to leave. I was hurt and it took a while to release all the pain around it, but I was better off in the long run with another huge lesson learned on the road to soulful leadership.

I learned so much about balancing time between business and work that needs to be done and family. I later acknowledged the gifts of Spirit to honour myself and be authentic to my wants and desires. I released the need to hold on to something that was not serving my soul and let it go. I acknowledged the gift of Insight into balancing my life and bringing harmony and flow, connecting myself to all things and not just one aspect, allowing myself to flow evenly between work and family. I also acknowledged the gift of Impulse, allowing my body to feel, move and sit with the pain so I could reflect through my lessons. I am grateful for the lesson that brought me closer to unlocking leadership potential through the soul, allowing soulful leadership to grow and expand.

Leadership is such a soulful process. It has the capacity to expand your growth. Leadership without soul is merely ego playing out its grandest fantasies without regard for purpose or people. For the evolution of humankind, leadership must contain three core elements or soul. We have moved on from the dictator, authoritarian tyrant leadership to more transformational leadership because it suits our soul purpose. Transformation is what our soul craves and leadership is the quickest way to transform your every being. You lead with your soul message that serves others and creates love and peace in your life.

Chapter 10: Activating The Three Core Elements for Leadership

"The most powerful weapon on Earth is the human soul on fire."
Ferdinand Foch

We now know that the life force or the three core elements are the essence of soulful leaders and are necessary to connect us to our soul. You might be thinking: why do we need to connect to our soul when leading? Think about it like this...would you leave your head behind if you were going out of your house or go to work naked? I thought not. Your soul is a part of you that is with you always but not always leading you as it was meant. The three core elements are the make up of your soul. It is your core and is meant to lead you into your leadership, whatever that may be for you. We have cut ourselves off from our core or soul so that we have separated each element as a piece and do not see it as a whole part of who we truly are and of what we are truly capable.

There are a million reasons why we should activate the three core elements to become soulful leaders, but I will give you my top five.

Authenticity

A soulful leader who has activated (whether conscious of it or not) their three core elements or soul will be in their authenticity actioning and speaking from a place of truth, clarity and reason.

Purpose

A soulful leader has divine purpose. Their ultimate purpose is in service to a greater good for human kind and not to their own ego. They are here to make a difference in the world and in the lives of those who choose to follow them.

Passion

A soulful leader oozes passion and this passion drives them to not give up on the divine purpose they know they were born to do. Their passion attracts like-minded individuals and ignites a ripple of passion in the hearts of those that listen or are in their presence.

Compassion

A soulful leader uses compassion as their mantra. Compassion is their virtue and is always at the forefront of decisions and actions made. A soulful leader's compassion is an extension of their authentic voice and action.

Wisdom

A soulful leader is filled with the wisdom of spirit. They understand themselves and are open to others revealing their truths to them to better their leadership capacity. A soulful leader's wisdom is aligned with their divine purpose. They are open to divine and spiritual guidance from those around them and their unseen divine guides. This wisdom brings another form of communication that is the soul connection (more in chapter 11).

For these five reasons alone, activating your three core elements for leadership is essential to being the best leader you can be.

How do we activate the three core elements, or blueprint when leading?

This is the million-dollar question. You can talk about it and tell everyone how great the three core elements are when activated, but how do you do it? It's simple, but it does take practice. You know how to activate each element separately by intentionally breathing into that area, so we do the same when we activate all three. The soul breathing exercise was channelled by divine guidance.

Soul breathing

Exercise #23

(Divine Exercise)

Breathe into the base of Impulse and feel the energy moving within.

Continue breathing and see the energy swirling in the base of Impulse.

Allow the breath to be moved by the energy of Impulse.

Slow your breathing into a soft and slow rhythm.

When you feel the full movement of the energy in Impulse, allow the energy to move up into Spirit.

Feel the opening of your heart expand as the two energies surge and mix together.

Slow your breathing into a soft and slow rhythm.

Breathe into your heart, allowing her to expand.

PART 7 - The Blueprint

Let her energy return home to Impulse and back up to the heart in a cyclic rhythm.

Allow the energy to be guided up toward Insight

Feel the V shape and the triangle at the front third eye brighten and pulsate with energy.

Send the energy to Spirit and home to Impulse and back up through Spirit and then Insight.

Allow this breathing to activate the soul connection.

_____

_____

_____

This soul breathing activation exercise will need lots of practise. When you are familiar with the feelings of each element being activated, it will get quicker each time. It can take seconds to activate when you have practised and are aware of the feeling of activating each element.

Before you go into work or a meeting, do your soul breathing and you will feel a heightened surge of energy, yet calming and clear (the best way I can describe the feeling). This is great before a presentation too.

Having the three elements activated before a meeting or when you go into work will give you a sense of calm and clarity when taking on tasks or discussing items on the agenda. When you feel the energy leave your body, take another moment to intentionally breathe and activate the soul. You may think this is hard work and time-consuming, but I would argue that lack of clarity and stress are more energy taxing and time wasters. Stress spreads a yucky energy that can consume the office or the workers around you. You notice this when you walk into some work places. You feel like you want to turn around and walk out. This is because of the negative energetic vibes that people emit sometimes without them knowing.

If you activate your soul and keep yourself in a container or contained about arm's width all the way around you, then it acts as a barrier to negative energies affecting you. I am very sensitive to energy and I can feel it in people and places and sometimes it's not a very nice feeling. When I haven't contained myself, I have felt nauseous and have been close to vomiting. Some people whose energy is low or negative feel prickly when I'm close to them. When this happens to me, I am always reminded to activate soul breathing and contain my energy.

A result from activating the three elements or the soul is you will emit a light, not seen by the human eye (unless you see auras), but people will notice a radiant look about you or be drawn to you in some way. This is the radiance that transformational leaders have. People are automatically drawn to you. Your leadership becomes magnetic and attracts the energy, resources and changes you want to see happen with little effort just soul.

When you speak from the soul, you do not need to find the right words to say. When I have found myself trying to find words in presentations or even just in conversations, I just breathe and let the words fall out. They make much more sense and you find yourself speaking of things and you wondered how did you know about that or where did that come from? Well, it comes form the all-knowing blueprint of our soul. When we allow it to freely flow, it will give us snippets of information that we need at the right moment.

Have you ever noticed when someone is positive or happy and how catchy that energy is? Activating the three core elements works the same way. Because you are connected to your soul, you will feel more balanced and at peace, maybe even happy and this will pour out from you, catching on

PART 7 - The Blueprint

to others and even filling up the environment that you are in. You will feel yourself wanting to stay away from people that bring your energy down. Keeping yourself contained around these people will help keep your energy balanced and can sometimes help their energy lift too, but this will depend on their situation and what's happening in their life.

Soul activated planning, actioning and goal setting

When you are getting ready to do strategic planning or setting targets in your business, organisation or even at home with your partner, activate your soul through the breathing exercise above and then follow the exercise below.

Exercise #24

(Divine Exercise)

Bring your intention for planning or goal setting into Spirit (heart).

Feel the energy swirling around your intention.

Send the intention to Impulse and feel the intention here.

Use the same intention for planning and goal setting into Insight (third eye).

Feel the energy swirling around your intention.

Send the intention to Impulse and feel it join with the same intention from Spirit.

Notice how they are the same but feel different, from a feminine and masculine essence.

Keep the intention in the Impulse and allow the creative energy to flow.

_____

_____

_____

Putting the same intention into Spirit and Insight allows the feminine and masculine essence to be present in your creativity. At the core of creativity is the union of feminine and masculine energy, as said in the creation story. When it comes to feminine and masculine essences in the workplace or at home, it looks like this:

Feminine Essence	**Masculine Essence**
Visualisation	Big Action
Creativity	Risk
Intuition	Structure
Trust	Force
Flexibility	Push
Go with the flow	To-do list
Listen	Detailed focus
Receive	Outcome driven
Feeling	Competitive

PART 7 - The Blueprint

A male or female can posses either feminine or masculine essences when it comes to work or play. We need to be balanced to manifest and create our ideal outcomes. Impulse is the element of creativity. It is where we birth and form takes shape from the feminine and masculine union. Contrary to the mind being our creativity centre, it is actually a combination of Insight and Spirit coming together in the area of Impulse and then sent back to Spirit and Insight to visualise and gain clarity. So bringing in the same intention from the feminine essence of Spirit and the masculine essence of Insight will bring in an energetic 50/50 balance to create and form ideas. From the list, you can see how too much of one essence can be either too airy-fairy, not getting much action done or to rigid, not allowing room for flexibility. It is the yin yang of balance.

You can gage how you work, either too feminine or too masculine. If you are unbalanced, things may seem like they never get done or others constantly let you down or you are constantly pushing and forcing things to get the results you want. A great intention to start with if you feel you are more of the feminine or masculine essence is to intend for more balance in planning and actioning.

I found when working in education I had more masculine energy, even though my friends would argue that I was more balanced. On reflection, since moving into business, I saw how working for someone made me more masculine in my approach to leadership. I was data and performance driven and everything was to push. Establishing my own businesses was a different ball game. I found myself spending too much time creating and not enough big action. I was getting into feeling and intuition rather than balancing it all out. Figuring out the key to how I worked and got stuff done was the beginning to balancing out the scales of manifesting the outcomes and visualising the things I desired most. Now I intend these things to happen through activating them within the three core elements.

Soul communication when working with people

This has to be my favourite form of communication because no words are needed. This type of communication is an ancient form of transmitting information that is telepathic, but I'm calling it soul communication because as soon as you say telepathic people believe they can't do it (which is a load of BS) because we all have the blueprint to prove we can. When communicating through the soul, we get a greater understanding of how someone truly feels and what he or she deeply desire. Soul communication drops our ego and judgements as soon as we are open. We become deeply focused on the truth we hear and see, even if they aren't apparent on the outside. Communicating this way allows us to feel the silver threads of connection that tie us to all living things.

The best reason to communicate this way when working with others is because people you work with will TRUST you. Relational trust in any relationship or workplace, especially when leading, is the number one essential. It's the difference between: do I want to hang in here or do I want to leave. People will stay in a relationship if they feel safe and safety is due to trust. Can I trust this person to be with them or follow their cause?

This is the essence of Spirit and Impulse that shines through this communication and it is Insight that processes the information back into the body. It is important to mention that Insight processes the information back to the body and does not analyse it in the brain. It is a full learning sensation using cognitive mindfulness in the process of soul communication. The communication flow in the body runs through a processing system. The information comes in through Insight (third eye, human eyes and ears) and in sensitive circumstances from Spirit too. The information is sent through Spirit (heart) and then to Impulse (union), where it is sensed or felt. All communication should be felt in Impulse, as this is an unbiased place. This is the practice of understanding sensory experiences within

PART 7 - The Blueprint

the body. Everything goes to the main energy centre of Impulse to find a resolution. When the resolution is found, it is sent back to Spirit and communicated from the heart. You hear this when people explain how that person spoke from the heart, it is through this process. It will become an automatic process when practiced regularly. Resolutions will always come when you activate the three core elements and if you need time, take all the time you need. It is perfectly fine to tell people that you need more time to let it sit. Notice how I said, "Let it sit," and not "Think about it"…we let things sit in Impulse and not in thought process.

The best thing is this communication evolves as your practice in using it evolves. Yes, it becomes telepathic or more like a soul reader unless someone, soul communicates back to you. The key with the advanced process to communication is to not use your head at all. This is a more complicated form of communication as it requires you to drop all judgement and ego, something humankind is evolving towards but still working on.

Begin from Impulse feeling everything around you straight into this energy centre. Then allow the sensory flow to go up to Spirit and flow.

When the souls are ready to communicate it will happen.

A screen similar to a cinema screen will appear. Do not judge and do not analyse, just allow shapes, pictures or sound to form or appear.

Communication…(divine message)

Using this communication requires a great deal of focus and love for humankind.

This love includes loving yourself.

Housing this pure energy comes from pure love.

Love you and the ones around you.

Allow the energy of love to flow through you when working with people.

Leave all ego, fear and judgement behind; do not let it walk with you.

Oh yes, I forgot to mention absolute love, thank you. Unconditional love for you is key to mastering soulful communication. Take your time developing this communication as it can take years. I do know, however, the awakened ones are doing things so much quicker, so focus and love will develop what you need at the right time.

PART 8

The Experience

Chapter 11:
Experiencing The Soul Connection

"If you want to conquer the anxiety of life, live in the moment, live in the breath."
Amit Ray

I participated in feminine leadership training with Rachael Jayne Groover in the Art of Feminine Presence and part of that training required a speaker training day as most of us had businesses. On this speaker training day, we were put through our paces facing our fears of stepping into the light and challenging ourselves out of our comfort zones. It was very liberating and inspiring. Our last speaking task was to deliver a three-minute pitch of our business with a call to action. Everyone including myself had written a quick pitch during our lunch break to be prepared for the afternoon's pitch fest.

Back at training, we were all told that we would be given a challenge that we had to do throughout our pitch. Some challenges were no smiling, don't use your hands, plant your feet in one spot, make serial eye contact and take longer pauses: the normal speaking challenges you might expect. However, my challenge was to throw out of my mind what I had just prepared for my pitch! No script, but feel into what the audience wants. I just about wet myself! A teacher being ill prepared for a presentation was not in my psyche. Boy was I challenged and I was speechless. So I closed my eyes, I activated Impulse (Mauri) and felt the energy expand. I then took the energy into Spirit (Mana) and felt the energy expand and connect with Impulse (Mauri). This took about three or four seconds, then I opened my eyes, looked at the audience of beautiful women and sent an intention to Insight (Maui) to give me the gift of hearing what they wanted.

PART 8 - The Experience

Within nanoseconds of giving Insight the intention, I felt the energy surge up through my body out through my third eye, which light up a screen just like the cinema and I heard voices that were coming from some of the women in the audience, except no-ones mouths were moving. I heard many voices calling out, "I'm a leader. I'm a soulful leader too." So I spoke to what I heard...

Hi, I'm Delvina Waiti and I am a Soulful Leader and.... (Screen came up) you are a soulful leader too.

And that was it! I didn't get to say anything else before bursting into tears and the audience clapping out of awe and excitement. What the hell just happened? I didn't realise that in that moment the audience could feel my experience and they had know idea what was going on, but they could feel the magic and power of what was being generated.

So let me tell you what I experienced and have been experiencing ever since.

When I got home from training, I meditated the next morning to ask my guides what happened to me. They told me I was given the gift of soul communication. My soul was connecting to the souls in the audience and even though I didn't say much, those that were around me could feel a powerful connection. They also showed me again how it works by circulating the energy through the three core elements, which together make up the soul when activated. I asked how do I know when I am connecting with some ones soul? The answer was that a black screen will appear and you will see or hear what their soul wants to communicate and even though the person may be telling you something different, the screen will show you the truth.

Wow! I was buzzing and couldn't wait to try it out. That's exactly what I did. I went back to The Art of Feminine Presence training that morning and

I did the energy circulation, activating the three core elements whenever I worked with someone and every time I connected, the screen came up and I could see what each person truly desired or was longing for. Now you might be thinking that only certain people have the gift of doing this type of communication, like a psychic or clairvoyant, but I am here to tell you that is not the case, and this whole book proves that I am here to teach those who are willing to learn to communicate from the soul.

You may be thinking: so what, I don't need to know what people's souls are communicating; but imagine being able to generate this energy as a leader, without saying much and you have an audience hanging on your every word, already sold on whatever you are selling or implement, through change. Pretty cool, I think and I want to help leaders to generate this type of communication in any industry that they are in because as I have been mentioning, these teachings are the universal blueprint that everyone is born with. You just need to unlock it. This used to be the way we communicated before spoken language came into our realm. We only spoke the truth, nothing was hidden and everyone cared. Very different from modern day communication, where you have to read between the lines and decipher intonations.

Soul connection...(divine message)

Communication is a soul connection that does not require thought or speech. It is a natural wave of energy that transmits outwards. Your soul is the transmitter and receiver. We give, we receive. Language was not meant to hurt or hold within the body. We hurt so many people by the words and actions we portray. Communication is only a wave. It comes and goes. It changes like the wind depending on your experiences. What your body experiences is the true communication to your soul. When we love the experience, we want to pass it on or transmit this feeling to others. We are a network, a network of experiential sensations giving and receiving, learning and teaching. You are a transmitter of truth, love and flow. Create your network of love and harmony. Be authentic and your network will thrive like a forest of trees connected to each other for survival.

Soul Wisdom

I am going to explain my soulful connection experience a little further for you, so you can grasp the expansiveness of this communication or soul wisdom. This is one of my five reasons for activating the three core elements in leadership purely because communication, is used 70-90% of the time when leading. A high percentage of that is communicated through non-verbal cues. In soul wisdom communication it is deciphering what is authentic, truthful and that usually comes from what is not being said or the way something is being communicated.

I have used a practice in a heart circle where you gage the level of energy that is being felt when someone communicates a desire, need or want to you. This is a powerful tool, and taken further or deeper into our essence and core, becomes soul wisdom, an awakened form of communication or an old form of telepathic communication. Yes, it is telepathic communication. Pretty cool to be able to break this down as a tool and use it for good. I believe it can only be used with pure intentions, otherwise it becomes distorted and interrupted, like a TV or radio signal that has white noise or a fuzzy screen.

We have lost the art of this ancient communication because of a shift in energy that came through different eras in time and space. This communication was also closed or shut off as a safety mechanism to those that wanted to keep the ancient and native wisdom pure, only opening a communication channel to Great Spirit. If it was that easy to do, everyone would be communicating through their soul, but we have lost so much connection to our body and our senses, making this communication very rear and difficult to establish. Fear of opening up to another or fear of your own thoughts being seen or felt is the reason this is so hard for us to do.

It is fear and ego that hinder all communication, including the everyday conversations we have with people in our lives. This stops you from speaking your true intentions for fear of being ridiculed or shut down. Sometimes we feed our egos by forcibly expressing our wants in a way that does not value anyone else but ourselves. The only way to build this communication muscle (and it is like a muscle) is by practicing and opening up to the awakened wisdom within. Using the practices within this book is a great place to begin exercising your spiritual wisdom and opening your heart.

When you communicate through the soul, nothing is hidden and our thoughts are pure and without ego. There is a mutual transition of truth and love, which is a form of unconditional understanding and by that I mean without judgement. When you hear a person's soul, you want so much to give them what they truly desire or want because you are connected to your soul at the same time. Our soul wants the simplest of pleasures that ignites more of our body and soul connection to spirit and our soul wants to make another soul happy too.

Experiencing Mindfulness

So lets talk about mindfulness. I love mindfulness and it has its place at a different tier or level. I started with mindfulness techniques and eventually got to soulfulness whilst delving deeper into my spirituality. I began meditating when I moved to Australia and dabbled in all sorts of other spiritual practices. Then I started sharing meditation techniques with my children and the children I was teaching in schools and some of my teaching colleagues before creating my first business. One of the successes in my life was teaching children self-worth and relaxation techniques as a course. I enjoyed watching children use these strategies in challenging and anxious times. I thought I really wanted to break out of the teaching industry and do Mindfulness for kids for the rest of my life.

When I did do this, I didn't get that joyous feeling I thought I would have. I did at first, but after a few sessions I started to see without guidance, each child was not carrying on the mindfulness practices even though I created videos and newsletters for parents to follow up with. Teachers did the same, just ticked the box on mindfulness and moved on to the next topic that needed to be covered. I understand that adults don't have the skills needed to take mindfulness any further, so I realised I needed to change the teachers or leaders to begin to help the kids. The Soulful Leader was born out of my passion to help children through life's challenges. I help teachers so they can lead by soulful example. Even as I write this book, I feel a different path opening as I have been teaching Native Wisdom through workshops and the people coming to me are here for their own soulful leadership journey.

Mindfulness is a stepping-stone that we can use to reach a soulful experience. Learning mindfulness techniques is just the start and can be any activity from Meditation, Yoga, Arts, Tantra (yes Tantra), Qi Gong, Tai Chi, and Reiki, etc. There are hundreds of options and the main things these mindfulness techniques have in common is focus and breath. So whatever helps you to focus and focus on your breathing is a form of mindfulness. Mindfulness helps us get into a state of understanding our connection to self and the environment we live in. Mindfulness techniques are necessary to activate the three core elements. Without focused breathing and focused intention or attention, it would take a lot longer to learn how to activate this energy.

Mindfulness is becoming a more accepted tool in mainstream education, even though many independent schools such as Kura Kaupapa (Maori

Immersion Schools) have been using mindfulness techniques through Karakia (prayer) and focused use of Maori Art forms for years. It is a way of indigenous life, as indigenous people understood their connection to all things through ancient knowledge and teachings. Indigenous people are in tune to the blueprint and the baskets pertaining to the knowledge of practice to activate the blueprint.

Schools are using forms of mindfulness with students, including meditation and yoga practices to help students regulate emotions and achieve more focused attention and learning in the classroom. I used meditation with students in grade prep (5-6 year olds) to help with beginning school anxieties such as separation anxiety and learning anxieties. The successes the students had were amazing, from no anxiety to knowing which mindfulness tool to use when feeling anxious or angry. It turned out to be a great tool for me as a teacher because I was able to see the students that had real learning difficulties as they would sleep during meditation rather than stay conscious. Two students in my time as a prep teacher would sleep constantly during after lunch meditation and both students were later discovered to have had serious medical conditions.

I began many wellbeing programs in school with success and received great feedback from parents noticing a behavioural change in their child on wellbeing day. I worked with grade 6 girls on mindfulness, preparing them for transition into high school and working on attitudes and images with the best results. These girls, once scatty and renowned for rumours amongst peers, became appreciative and tolerant of each other. Student welfare issues dropped and the girls knew how to deal with issues that arose.

The second half of the year I worked with grade 6 boys on building character. We watched inspirational clips about men and discussed the role models in their lives and we did tribal meditation. It was like an initiation into the tribe of men through meditation. I honestly thought I wasn't getting through to these boys until a parent came to me and said, "I just realised my son was doing meditation with you because I asked him why he was so calm on Thursday afternoons as opposed to the rest of the week. He told me that Mrs Waiti takes us for meditation in the afternoon. Thank you so much. I have noticed a huge difference in his behaviour." Five other parents came with similar responses and gratitude. I realised boys take things in differently, by action, so you need to watch them, compared to how open and verbal girls are with their experiences. These experiences with kids inspired me to take the leap and get this message out into the world.

Experiencing Soulfulness

Soul wisdom is just one experience in soulfulness. Through my own journey, I have come to realise the stepping-stones or paths needed to attain such profound and soulful experiences. I want to explain these paths as to help those that are seeking the same spiritual enlightenment. Our soulful journey or spiritual path is like steps and in my culture, we depict this as a stairway to the heavens. It ascends because our soul is always working to ascension back to Great Spirit or the Creator. Of course, along our human spiritual experiences and living life's challenges, it is not a simple climb. In the beginning of our spiritual journey, each lesson may take a long path or road trip before we can take the next step up. These roads can take years, months or sometimes weeks before we can move on our spiritual journey.

Just to make it a little more interesting, some roads have tests to ensure you have consolidated the learning before moving on. It takes work and I call it work because it's an intentional awareness that you need to keep in check all the time. It is a responsibility that we promised to Great Spirit before our journey to Earth. Yes, I fall off the bandwagon sometimes and I don't beat myself up like I used to. I understand the greater meaning of experiencing and sensing human challenges. I know that I had an experience and I get back up and carry on with my work.

When you begin your spiritual journey, it is new and exciting, filled with wonder and mysticalness. The key is having the right teachers to learn from. I have been blessed with the teachers I have had in my journey on the physical and spiritual planes. I appreciated those who brought me to this time and place as we do not get here alone without guidance. I remember thinking at one point in my spiritual journey that I knew a lot and felt rather proud of that. The more I learnt, the more I realised that I knew nothing and I became more humble in my learning and teaching of this work.

The key in that lesson is to keep learning, always staying keen and open as a student. When learning in the beginning, immerse yourself in as much knowledge as you can until you find what resonates with your soul. When you come into alignment with your soul's purpose, you can begin to channel your learning into the areas that interest you or are in your soul's purpose. In experiencing all these wonderful new things, you are enriching your senses on a higher level. Your calling will become apparent when you begin your soulful journey.

The soulful experience is so simple once you attain it and the message that streams in with this experience is pure and effervescent LOVE. Nothing else and nothing more needed. Your questions are answered for you in such simple yet profound ways that enhance your gratitude and appreciation for life. Beauty is entwined in love and experiences, are more joyous and appreciative, even the not so good experiences because you have gained an insight into the greater and grander scheme of learning, leadership and life. Your perspective is forever changed and you tend not to travel along the long roads of spiritual enlightenment because every experience is enlightenment. Every stone and pebble is an experiential learning to understand you better. Why do you need to understand yourself better? So that you can experience a rich and full life through the way you choose to lead it. In understanding yourself, you also help those around you take leadership in their lives and live with purpose.

Chapter 12:
The Soulful Journey Begins

"Becoming a soulful leader is about the life you choose to lead for your soul's purpose. Our souls are on an evolutionary journey too."
Delvina Waiti

Once you commit to the journey of a soulful leader, your world is never the same. A new door opens to a new world. Your heart opens and your body sings to be free. Free of limiting beliefs and rules that do not serve your creativity or the purpose of your creation. Your body becomes your Mecca of insight and intuition that you lead with in this world. It may sound woo-woo and airy-fairy, but it is exactly what happened to me. I stopped eating meat (only eating fish); I listen to my body more and live a healthier lifestyle. Simple things bring me amazing amounts of joy and happiness. I am more tolerant of the people in my life. I understand that I am blessed in so many ways.

This soulful journey has helped me love and honour all that I am and the gifts I create in my life, including my children and my relationships with those I love. When I love and honour myself through my soul, I am blessed with happiness and a motivation to serve and help others find the same soul connection. These feelings have engulfed me, all while trying to get my business off the ground, taking care of four and half kids (three in high school, one toddler and another on the way), on one wage (my husband's) and living with my parents (yes living with my parents!).

So I didn't start off skipping through a green field of daisies. In fact, I was stressed about money, having four kids and one wage. I lacked confidence in my business; being seen and heard scared the shit out of me. And I desperately wanted my own home; living with your parents is not ideal when you have a different belief system to parenting than the one you were brought up with. My soulful leader journey has lifted me to a place of clarity and blessings where I can see the same life but with a whole new lens, a soul lens. I have so much confidence in the message I am bringing to the world and I am openly receiving the abundance that comes with stepping into the spotlight, being seen and heard. My parents are a huge part of my soulful leader journey that I have learnt to stand up for what I believe in and change the energy dynamics by purely leading from the soul. Your journey will be different for you, but I guarantee the benefits are great, so great it changes your life.

The Soulful Leader Lenses

The soulful lens is the way you see the world and the way you see your life playing out before your eyes. You know when you are awakening to the soulful journey because your lens, the way you view the world around you, begins to change. You will experience gratitude in all life's challenges, experience love in all things and with love you will see beauty all around you. Physically you will change. You will look happier, calm, less stressed and even younger. The Soulful Leader journey is a fountain of youth and why not when you are following your purpose and doing things that make your heart sing. I know I would pay for a prescription of soulful lenses.

Leadership have various lenses in theory and practice. There are ethical leadership lenses, lenses of visionary leaders, intentional leadership lenses and the list goes on. Lenses are ways leaders of organisations can macro, and micro-manage organisational structure and functions. Lenses are necessary to ground yourself in the process and functioning of your purpose. Your business, organisation or life has a purpose and lenses keep your purpose in check and progressing along with minimal hiccups or challenges. Soulful Leadership too has lenses that keep us in check and progressing towards our purpose.

The Soulful Leadership Framework (SLF)

The soulful leader lenses entwined with soulful leadership strategies is called the Soulful Leadership Framework (SLF) that guides and encourages those leaders in professions to lead in a transformational, purposeful and impactful way. This framework is based on the 5 Processes of Soulful Leadership that Soulful Leaders go through in order to establish soulful leadership within their lives or organisation. This is how we map our journey as leaders, making sure we are authentic, ethical and soulful in all our actions and decisions.

The 5 Processes are what ground us into the physical world and our interactions with others towards our personal purpose or our organisational identity. It is such a valuable grounding tool for organising our thinking, information gathering, and communication. When we have clarity around our organising and thinking we can clearly communicate to others our intentions for the organisation or our lives. This framework and the lenses can help leaders through problems to solutions including the implementation of change and change management. The framework mastered becomes a multi-dimensional tool for all aspects of leadership, management, and coaching.

The multi-faceted nature of this framework and the processes require another book and workshops alone to explain and use in detail. That is what is planned for the near future. There are other lenses and processes that layer the framework in order for it to work in management and implementation stages of leadership. For now, I will give you a glimpse into the framework and give you a start on mapping your personal soulful journey through each of the processes. This is the foundational process

PART 8 - The Experience

only by which to build upon with soulful leader guidance and coaching towards your organisational or life mastery goals.

The Soulful Leadership Framework

- 5 Processes of Soulful Leadership

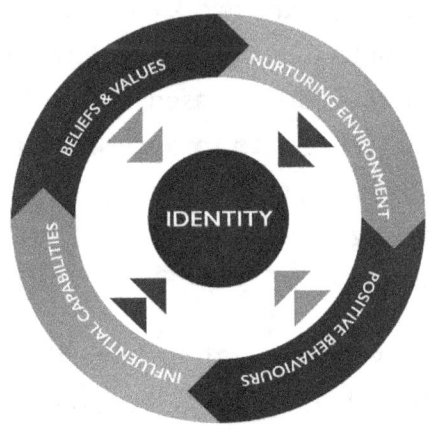

Mapping Your Soulful Leader Journey

Mapping your journey as a soulful leader keeps your accountable, especially when we keep telling ourselves that we are going to do something and it never happens or we find never ending excuses why it hasn't happened yet. This can be used as a personal tracker to ensure all aspects of your progress and development are shifting towards your goals or purpose. Personal use is the simplest use of the SLF. Each process needs to be accounted for in mapping your journey. Working with all 5 Processes in unity creates soulful harmonious balance in achieving your purpose. You can begin at any process, but the questioning is done in two layers: Pinpoint (highlights the issue) and Flashlight (brings a light to the issue). By asking ourselves certain simple questions, we begin to map our soulful journey.

The beauty of being able to have a tool to map our foundations is we can clearly identify an area within the process that needs work or has gaps in it. Understanding these gaps helps us to put these under a microscope to further process why certain aspects of our life or business are not going as planned. Each of these processes includes practical and actionable exercises to enable each gap to be filled with the right action and the right soulful intention, leaving no stone unturned when building a strong foundation to build your life or empire upon.

Taking the next step

The awakening of the soulful leader revolution is such a powerful message that I believe even in this book I have only scratched the surface. I believe the journey of each individual is unique and sharing each of our soulful awakened experiences is what our true soul journey is about. We learn so much through a collective resonant connection and as we learn together, we raise a conscious global vibration of light energy that increases more awareness. Awareness of life lessons and our reaction to them, awareness of our environment and the impact on how we show up in the world, awareness of people we keep company with and awareness of our soul purpose and our connection to all of it. Becoming a soulful leader is more about the life you choose to lead for your soul's purpose. Our souls are on an evolutionary journey too.

You now have the practices and tools to begin enriching your life along your Soulful Leader journey.

What is calling you right now?

Take action on that feeling and I promise you it will be one of the most profound journeys you will embark on. Soulful Leadership is the journey to self-discovery, self-perseverance and purposefulness. You are the Soulful Leader this new world is calling for...

PART 8 - The Experience

So what is calling you right now?

Your next step is to feel into the call that has been nagging and tugging at you like a toddler at your side. Feel into the one thing that keeps you wondering, dreaming and pondering…

I wonder what would happen if I did what I loved?

If it is something that makes your heart sing, then ponder no more and take charge. Your soul is urging you to set yourself free so that you can live the life or have the business that makes your heart skip a beat.

You are the Soulful Leader this world needs.

We need professionals willing to break out of the conformity that restricts feeling, emotion and heart from everyday interactions with people and services that are provided. We need teachers willing to teach outside the norm of confined and rigid thinking. We need big corporations to build empires that give back to worlds less fortunate than themselves. The world is ready for this change, and the earth is in perfect alignment to engage Soulful Leaders ready to hear their calling.

What is calling you right now?

This is a bold move and it's not always easy. If it were, the world would be full of people dreaming, living and loving life on purpose. But the joy and lessons are only learnt in the journey and not on the silver platter at the end. The lessons and answers are in the uncomfortableness, the uncertainty and the pain. It is what stretches us to think and act beyond our comfort zone. Nelson Mandela beautifully quoted, "Do not judge me by my successes, judge me by how many times I fell down and got back up again." Soulful inspiration is in the essence of Time and Change - The learning of becoming.

Invest in yourself; invest in your soul because you are worth the investment. It takes inner strength to stand out for what you believe in and at times you may feel alone, but I assure you, you are never alone. Gather support for your soulful journey. Get a mentor and follow the strategies and tools in this book. Surround yourself with positive and inspirational materials and tell yourself each day how grateful you are for the gifts you own and the gifts you will serve with.

Make your mark, create your legacy and listen to the song in your heart.

Lead from the SOUL.

Author and Divine Guidance Message

Illuminate your Soul

You are awakened. Your time is now and this book has shown you how. You know how to illuminate your soul and you know how great it feels. The world needs your luminescence and your leadership. Lead from your Spirit, Impulse and Insight knowing that you are where you are meant to be...

Let your feet walk in the footprints of other soulful leaders.

Feel their presence lift you up into the sunlight.

Know that you are the soulful presence that is laying foundations for those to come behind you.

You are where you are meant to be.

Your true self, your soul needs to shine.

Lead from the heart, lead from the soul

Walk with the divine.

Don't let the business of life dim your soul light.

Let the creativity of life light you up.

Bring to love all that you love to keep the light lit.

No challenge is too great. It just needs looking at from a different point of view.

Go forth and walk the soulful path

Others will follow your light, your truth, your love.

Give yourself only to you.

Let go of all that does not serve you.

Honour your wholeness, your divineness

Be who you came here to be.

I love it when divine knowledge appears at the right time (which it has throughout this book). I am always grateful. So as the divine ones have said, go and rock this world with your soulfulness. Awaken everyone in your presence with your light and knowledge. Challenges are just blessings in disguise, so give them to your soul and you will see it for the blessing it truly is. Always remember you are never alone in this journey. There are many souls opening up in this world. Just call out: your soul will hear and divine guidance will be with you.

Soulful Love

Delvina Waiti

The Soulful Leader

Acknowledgments

My life has significantly changed through the process of writing this book. Energetically I feel revitalised and nurtured; physically I feel nourished and supported and emotionally I am celebrating another milestone reached in my life. I am celebrating and acknowledging the wonderful support around me in getting to this achievement. To my amazing family, I am glad we chose each other to ride the soul train together. I love my parents for supporting me and watching my little one while I sat in my car and wrote. To my beautiful kids, thank you for keeping me on my toes by asking everyday, "How's your book going, Mum?" To my beautiful husband, thank you for letting me follow my dreams and desires. To my beautiful BFF, thank you for believing in me and encouraging me to keep going. To every divine guide that dropped in a message, I am eternally grateful and friggen ecstatic because that was the best experience ever!

About The Author

Delvina Waiti is an author, speaker and soulful leader with a prodigious passion to bring a soulful leadership revolution to the world. Creating her soul-purpose driven business as "Delvina Waiti – The Soulful Leader" she is dedicated to delivering training and soul wisdom to men and women ready for personal leadership growth.

With a background in Education and Masters in Leadership, Delvina has forged her business through her passion to deliver profound, transformational and personal leadership training to inspire her dreams of a soulful leadership revolution. Her book "Native Wisdom of a Soulful Leader – Understanding the 3 core elements to accessing the leader within" is the first rendition of her soul wisdom leadership revelations. The wisdom in her book is deep rooted in ancient perspectives of leadership and the true human potential we all hold as leaders of the New World.

There are many more books seeding in the garden of soul wisdom waiting for the right time to germinate into the world.

Delvina's New Zealand Maori ethnic background is the foundation for her deep soul wisdom. Her ancestral connections continue to guide her through profound understandings of human potential, creativity and unconditional love. From a young age Delvina has always been guided by the spirit world of her people and continues to pass this knowledge on through her book and soul wisdom training through a universal understanding.

"Becoming a soulful leader is about the life you choose to lead for your souls purpose. Our souls are on an evolutionary journey too."
Delvina Waiti

www.ingramcontent.com/pod-product-compliance
Lightning Source LLC
Chambersburg PA
CBHW070619300426
44113CB00010B/1586